SCHOLASTIC

TIMES TABLES

TEACHER'S BOOK

AGES 5–7

Scholastic Education, an imprint of Scholastic Ltd

Book End, Range Road, Witney, Oxfordshire, OX29 0YD

Registered office: Westfield Road, Southam, Warwickshire CV47 0RA

www.scholastic.co.uk

© 2018, Scholastic Ltd

1 2 3 4 5 6 7 8 9   8 9 0 1 2 3 4 5 6 7

British Library Cataloguing-in-Publication Data

A catalogue record for this book is available from the British Library.

ISBN 978-1407-18272-8

Printed and bound by Bell and Bain Ltd, Glasgow

Author
Louise Carruthers

Editorial
Rachel Morgan, Shannon Keenlyside, Audrey Stokes, Helen Lewis and Gemma Smith

Cover and Series Design
Scholastic Design Team: Nicolle Thomas, Neil Salt and Alice Duggan

Layout
Claire Green

Illustrations
Gaynor Barrs

CONTENTS

Scholastic Times Tables

The National Curriculum in England expects all children to be taught to recall the multiplication and division facts for multiplication tables up to 12 × 12. From June 2020, all children in England will also take an online timed multiplication tables check, up to and including 12 × 12, at the end of Year 4. This means that, more than ever, a firm grasp of the times tables is key.

It is important to keep in mind that, for many children, the time spent trying to master the times tables may define how they view themselves as mathematicians. A focus on rapid recall can increase anxiety, not only with multiplication, but with other areas of maths. Conversely, rapid recall of times tables can be confused with deep understanding of multiplication and division; children may move on to new concepts too quickly, causing problems in understanding later on.

These factors make it all the more important that we get right how we teach, and how children learn, the times tables. *Scholastic Times Tables* provides a wealth of rich and varied activities in the *Teacher's Book* and engaging recaps and practice in the *Practice Book*. These work alongside our diagnostic and timed digital practice to help you and your children not only reach National Curriculum expectations but develop a deep understanding of multiplication. The following strategies should be used to get the best results.

Building understanding

- ***Provide opportunities for exploration and reasoning*** *Scholastic Times Tables Teacher's Book* offers a rich variety of activities to get your children thinking about the times tables in a meaningful way. Children should explore ideas, building on what they already know to develop a deeper understanding of multiplication. The *Practice Book* offers varied practice as well as providing further opportunities to develop their problem-solving and reasoning skills (see page 7).

- ***Represent multiplication visually*** When exploring any multiplication table, it is important that children are continually exposed to the different ways in which multiplication can be represented, such as number lines, arrays, counters, number frames, number rods and base-10 equipment. Use these throughout Key Stage 1 **and** 2 as part of your whole-class teaching. Encourage children of **all abilities** to use them to model and check their work as well as explore ideas and patterns.

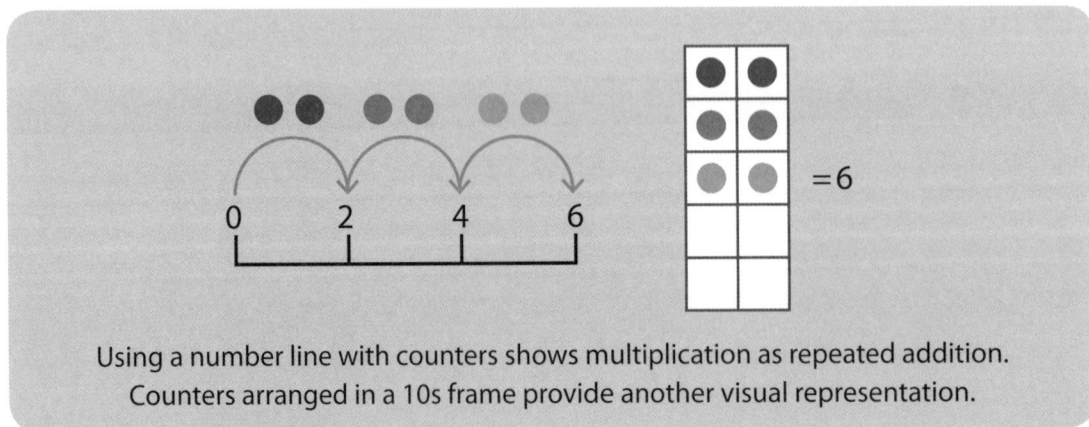

Using a number line with counters shows multiplication as repeated addition.
Counters arranged in a 10s frame provide another visual representation.

- ***Promote talk and discussion*** Many of the activities in this book, as well as the *Practice Book*, ask children to explore an idea and explain their thinking. Shift the focus away from talking only when you think you know the 'right' answer, by explaining that talking is a great way to work through a problem as it helps us work out what we do and do not know. Sharing your ideas with someone else is even better!

- **Find patterns and draw connections** Move away from talking about 'tricks' and making things 'easy' (for example *Multiplying by 10? Easy! Put a 0 on it!*) and instead focus on finding patterns and using what you already know to build understanding. Allow children to discover and test these patterns themselves, finding out what works and what doesn't. For example *2 × 4, 4 × 4, 8 × 4. What do you notice? Could you use this to predict the answer of 16 × 4?*

- **Use what they know to learn more** Building on the connections in the tables, we suggest introducing the tables in the following order. Continue to emphasise these links even after all the tables have been introduced.

Key Stage 1			Lower Key Stage 2							
2 ×	**5 ×**	**10 ×**	**4 ×**	**8 ×**	**3 ×**	**6 ×**	**7 ×**	**9 ×**	**11 ×**	**12 ×**
			(linked to 2 ×)	(linked to 2 × and 4 ×)	(linked to 2 ×)	(linked to 3 ×)	(linked to 6 ×)	(linked to 10 ×)	(linked to 10 ×)	(linked to 10 × and 2 ×)

Developing rapid recall

- **Practise in short bursts, often** Rather than devoting a longer chunk of time to rehearsing the times tables, aim to fit short sessions of practice into your day. Even a minute is enough time to fit in a quick all-class chant of a times table.

- **Make it fun** Use engaging and low-stress activities to encourage children to commit their times tables to memory, building their confidence and fluency. For example challenge children to set the times tables to music or make up a times tables rap!

- **Keep it bubbling** Children will use the times tables across many areas of maths and in everyday life. Continue to revisit them even when you think they have learned them by heart.

- **Carefully consider when to test** Timed practice can be stressful for many children. Reiterate that understanding is most important and that speed will come with time and practice. Provide opportunities for low-stakes timed practice; this will help them to get used to being tested without the fear of failure. Challenge children to compete against their own personal best time rather than against that of others.

The components

Teacher's Book

The *Scholastic Times Tables Teacher's Book* provides you with a wealth of activities to help your children master the times tables. Work through the activities one by one or dip in and out – whatever works best for you and your class!

Choose from a bank of activities which promote problem-solving, reasoning and fluency. Aim to use a range of activities so that children have an opportunity to approach the times tables in a variety of ways.

The activities use a wide range of resources: some rely on using concrete resources, others have a whiteboard component to them, and others may require a photocopiable resource which can be downloaded from www.scholastic.co.uk/timestables-resources. Finally, some require no resources at all.

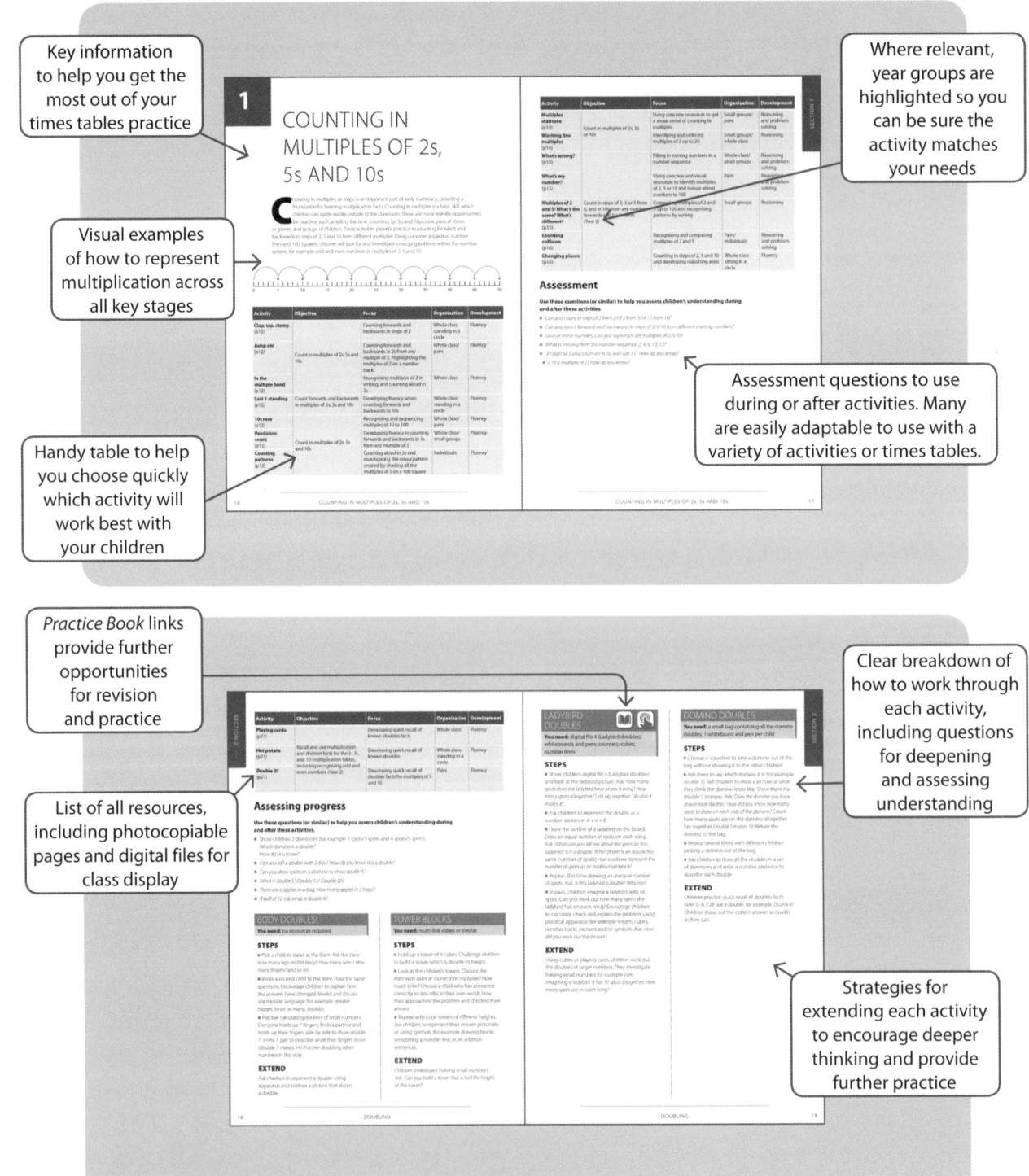

Key information to help you get the most out of your times tables practice

Where relevant, year groups are highlighted so you can be sure the activity matches your needs

Visual examples of how to represent multiplication across all key stages

Handy table to help you choose quickly which activity will work best with your children

Assessment questions to use during or after activities. Many are easily adaptable to use with a variety of activities or times tables.

Practice Book links provide further opportunities for revision and practice

Clear breakdown of how to work through each activity, including questions for deepening and assessing understanding

List of all resources, including photocopiable pages and digital files for class display

Strategies for extending each activity to encourage deeper thinking and provide further practice

The *Practice Book*

The *Scholastic Times Tables Practice Book* has been designed to provide children with further opportunities for revision and practice of the times tables.

Use it alongside the *Teacher's Book*, as part of general class practice or for home learning. Look for the *Practice Book* icon 📖 in the 'You will need' section at the start of an activity for activities which relate directly to the *Times Tables Practice Book*.

> Each unit focuses on a different topic or times table.

> This section provides children with the opportunity to revisit what they have learned with visual examples to support their understanding.

> Children should work through the questions in order for varied practice which builds in difficulty.

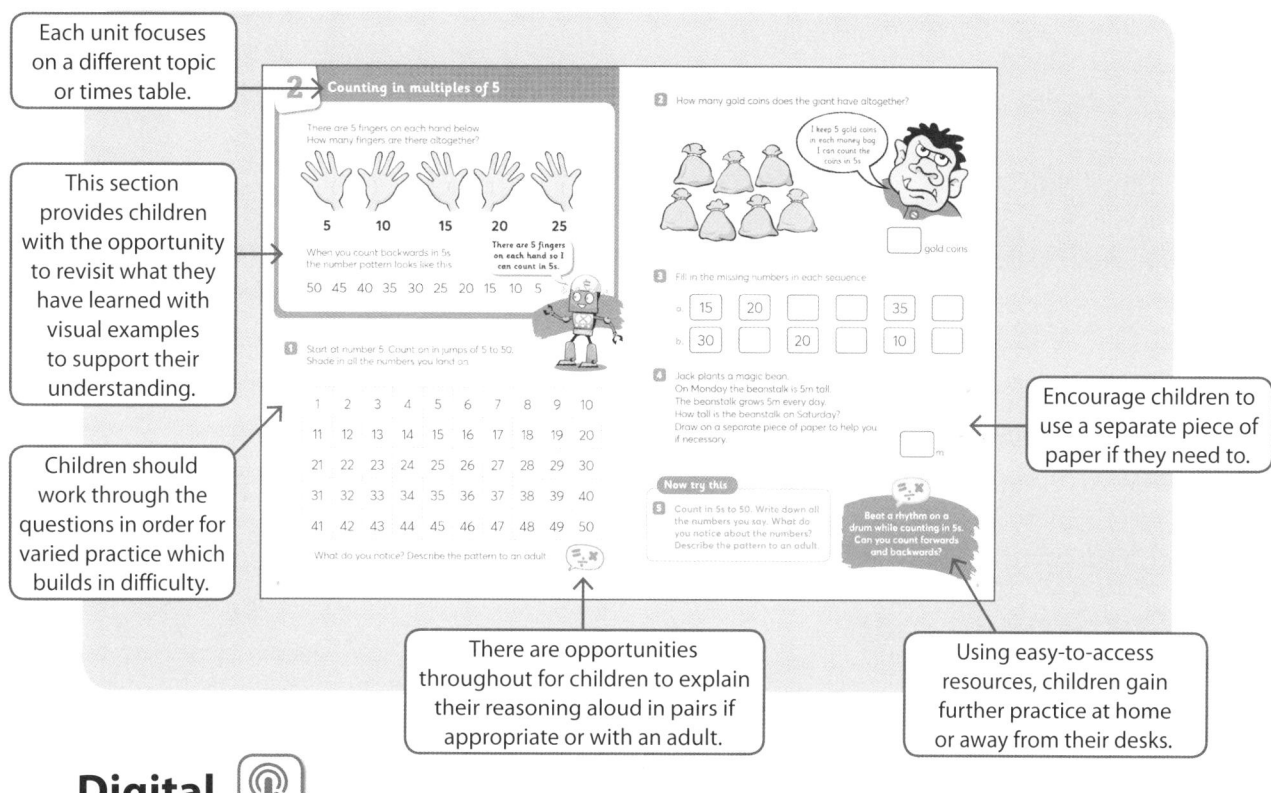

> Encourage children to use a separate piece of paper if they need to.

> There are opportunities throughout for children to explain their reasoning aloud in pairs if appropriate or with an adult.

> Using easy-to-access resources, children gain further practice at home or away from their desks.

Digital 📲

Additional materials for this book can be found online at the following address: **www.scholastic.co.uk/timestables-resources** these include:

- resource pages including games and worksheets
- supporting PowerPoint digital files for display during your classroom teaching
- quick-fire written tests for additional practice or homework. These tests have three levels of differentiation and are aligned with a unit or group of units from the *Teacher's Book*. Assign one of the three sections at a time and progress through them in order.

If digital files are required, they will be listed in the 'You will need' section at the start of an activity. Look for the digital icon 📲 for activities using digital content.

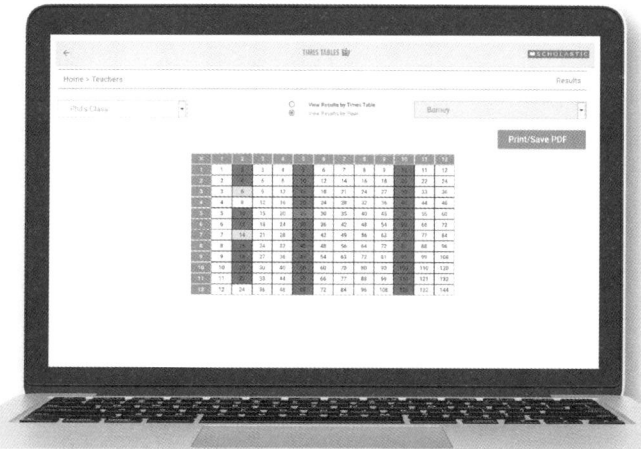

The digital *Times Tables Check* is included on a USB stick as part of the Classroom Pack, it follows the format of the National Times Tables Check. It can be used to inform your teaching and to provide practice in the test format. Frequently dipping in and out of the program will allow you to gauge progress as well as improving children's familiarity and reducing any associated anxiety that may arise from such checks.

The *Times Tables Check* is customisable, allowing you to select which times tables you would like to include in the check (1–12), the number of questions given and how long children have to complete it. Set up your class then adjust the class settings or individual settings to tailor the check to your children's needs. Use the reporting features to track children's progress and pinpoint areas for additional support. In addition, there is a practice area for children to explore which is not tracked in the reporting area.

The teacher settings are password protected with the password: **login**. A full how to use guide can be found on the USB stick or in the teacher's area of the program.

To install the content, insert the USB stick into a USB port on your computer.
For Windows users, if the install program does not start automatically, navigate to the USB drive, double click the installer program icon and follow the instructions.

For Mac users, navigate to the USB drive and double click the disk image file on the USB drive to mount it. In the window that opens, drag the application file icon to the applications folder icon.

Recommended system requirements:
USB type A port
Windows 7 and later are supported
MacOS 10.9 and above are supported (64bit only)
An internet connection is required for some program features.

Curriculum map

Scholastic Times Tables has been designed to meet the aims of the National Curriculum for mathematics in England to ensure that all pupils:

- become **fluent** in the fundamentals of mathematics, including through varied and frequent practice with increasingly complex problems over time, so that pupils develop conceptual understanding and the ability to recall and apply knowledge rapidly and accurately
- **reason mathematically** by following a line of enquiry, conjecturing relationships and generalisations, and developing an argument, justification or proof using mathematical language
- can solve **problems** by applying their mathematics to a variety of routine and non-routine problems with increasing sophistication, including breaking down problems into a series of simpler steps and persevering in seeking solutions

Mathematics is an interconnected subject in which pupils need to be able to move fluently between representations of mathematical ideas. The programmes of study are, by necessity, organised into apparently distinct domains, but pupils should make rich connections across mathematical ideas to develop fluency, mathematical reasoning and competence in solving increasingly sophisticated problems. They should also apply their mathematical knowledge to science and other subjects.

The expectation is that the majority of pupils will move through the programmes of study at broadly the same pace. However, decisions about when to progress should always be based on the security of pupils' understanding and their readiness to progress to the next stage. Pupils who grasp concepts rapidly should be challenged through being offered rich and sophisticated problems before any acceleration through new content. Those who are not sufficiently fluent with earlier material should consolidate their understanding, including through additional practice, before moving on.

The activities in this book cover the Programme of Study (statutory requirements) in Number: Multiplication and division for the following year groups:

Year 1

Pupils should be taught to:

- solve 1-step problems involving multiplication and division, by calculating the answer using concrete objects, pictorial representations and arrays with the support of the teacher

Year 2

Pupils should be taught to:

- recall and use multiplication and division facts for the 2-, 5- and 10-multiplication tables, including recognising odd and even numbers
- calculate mathematical statements for multiplication and division within the multiplication tables and write them using the multiplication ($\times$), division ($\div$) and equals ($=$) signs
- show that multiplication of 2 numbers can be done in any order (commutative) and division of 1 number by another cannot
- solve problems involving multiplication and division, using materials, arrays, repeated addition, mental methods, and multiplication and division facts, including problems in contexts

1

COUNTING IN MULTIPLES OF 2s, 5s AND 10s

Counting in multiples, or steps, is an important part of early numeracy, providing a foundation for learning multiplication facts. Counting in multiples is a basic skill which children can apply readily outside of the classroom. There are many real-life opportunities for practice, such as telling the time, counting 2p, 5p and 10p coins, pairs of shoes or gloves, and groups of children. These activities provide practice in counting forwards and backwards in steps of 2, 5 and 10 from different multiples. Using concrete apparatus, number lines and 100 squares, children will look for and investigate emerging patterns within the number system, for example odd and even numbers or multiples of 2, 5 and 10.

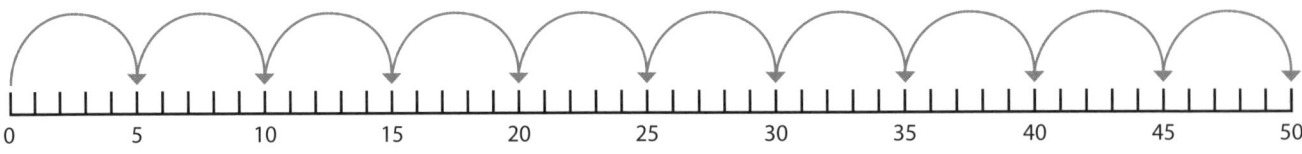

Activity	Objective	Focus	Organisation	Development
Clap, tap, stamp (p12)		Counting forwards and backwards in steps of 2	Whole class standing in a circle	Fluency
Jump on! (p12)	Count in multiples of 2s, 5s and 10s	Counting forwards and backwards in 2s from any multiple of 2. Highlighting the multiples of 2 on a number track.	Whole class/pairs	Fluency
In the multiple band (p12)		Recognising multiples of 2 in writing, and counting aloud in 2s	Whole class	Fluency
Last 1 standing (p12)	Count forwards and backwards in multiples of 2s, 5s and 10s	Developing fluency when counting forwards and backwards in 10s	Whole class standing in a circle	Fluency
10s race (p13)		Recognising and sequencing multiples of 10 to 100	Whole class/pairs	Fluency
Pendulum count (p13)	Count in multiples of 2s, 5s and 10s	Developing fluency in counting forwards and backwards in 5s from any multiple of 5	Whole class/small groups	Fluency
Counting patterns (p13)		Counting aloud in 5s and investigating the visual pattern created by shading all the multiples of 5 on a 100 square	Individuals	Fluency

Activity	Objective	Focus	Organisation	Development
Multiples staircase (p14)	Count in multiples of 2s, 5s or 10s	Using concrete resources to get a visual sense of counting in multiples	Small groups/ pairs	Reasoning and problem-solving
Washing line multiples (p14)		Identifying and ordering multiples of 2 up to 20	Small groups/ whole class	Reasoning
What's wrong? (p15)		Filling in missing numbers in a number sequence	Whole class/ small groups	Reasoning and problem-solving
What's my number? (p15)		Using concrete and visual resources to identify multiples of 2, 5 or 10 and reason about numbers to 100	Pairs	Reasoning and problem-solving
Multiples of 2 and 5: What's the same? What's different? (p15)	Count in steps of 2, 3 or 5 from 0, and in 10s from any number forwards and backwards (Year 2)	Comparing multiples of 2 and 5 up to 100 and recognising patterns by sorting	Small groups	Reasoning
Counting collision (p16)		Recognising and comparing multiples of 2 and 5	Pairs/ individuals	Reasoning and problem-solving
Changing places (p16)		Counting in steps of 2, 5 and 10 and developing reasoning skills	Whole class sitting in a circle	Fluency

Assessment

Use these questions (or similar) to help you assess children's understanding during and after these activities.

- *Can you count in steps of 2 from 2/of 5 from 5/of 10 from 10?*
- *Can you count forwards and backwards in steps of 2/5/10 from different starting numbers?*
- *Look at these numbers. Can you say which are multiples of 2/5/10?*
- *What is missing from this number sequence: 2, 4, 6, 10, 12?*
- *If I start at 5 and count on in 5s, will I say 31? How do you know*
- *Is 10 a multiple of 2? How do you know?*

CLAP, TAP, STAMP

PAGES 6 AND 7

You need: no resources required

STEPS

■ Ask children to watch and then join in with a simple 4-beat rhythm – clap both hands together, tap knees, stamp 1 foot and then the other. Once a steady rhythm is established, lead the class counting from 0 in 2s on each clap and staying silent on the other actions; this will give children time to think of the next number.

■ Repeat several times. As children become more confident, try counting in 2s on every action.

■ Now try counting back in 2s from 20.

EXTEND

Children count in 2s beyond 20. Devise other action sequences for them to practise counting forwards and backwards in steps of 5 and 10.

JUMP ON!

You need: resource 1 (Jump on!); a small toy per pair (for example a compare bear)

STEPS

■ Lead the whole class jumping up and down on the spot while counting in 2s to 20 or beyond.

■ Choose different children to come to the front to count in 2s as far as they can while doing, for example star jumps, frog jumps, fast/slow jumps.

■ Give each pair resource 1 (Jump on!) and a bear. Children place the bear on 0 and practise counting on and back in 2s. Say: *Put your bear on number 16. Where will it land on its next jump? Start on 12 and jump back 3 jumps of 2. Where do you land?* Introduce the word 'multiple'.

■ Children colour all the numbers where the bear lands on their number track. Discuss the pattern of odd and even numbers. *What do you notice about the multiples of 2?* (they are all even)

EXTEND

Adapt the activity to practise counting in 5s or 10s. Children can investigate counting in 2s and the pattern of odd and even numbers on a 100 square.

IN THE MULTIPLE BAND

You need: a selection of small percussion instruments; number cards (even numbers 2–20)

STEPS

■ Invite 10 children to come to the front and choose an instrument and a number card. Give them a number card. The card will indicate when they should play their instrument.

■ As a class, count on in 2s from 2. Explain that whenever children in the band hear their number, they should play their instrument. Before beginning, ask: *Who has the number that is 2 more than 2? What number comes next? And after that 1? How many is 2 more than this number?*

■ Work slowly through all multiples of 2 up to 20 a number of times so children become comfortable with the pattern and gain confidence in their timings.

EXTEND

Play again but give children more than 1 card each. Extend beyond 20. Ask children to perform an action for each multiple. Adapt the activity to practise counting in 5s or 10s.

LAST 1 STANDING

PAGES 10 TO 11

You need: a beanbag; resource (100 square) or a number track (optional)

STEPS

■ Choose a child to hold the beanbag.

■ Ask children to pass the beanbag around the circle while counting on in 10s from 0. The child holding the beanbag when 100 is reached must sit down. They are out of the game but should keep counting with the rest of the class.

■ Then ask children to count on and back from different multiples of 10, using a 100 square or number track if necessary. Whoever is holding the beanbag when 0 or 100 are reached must sit down. Ask: *Can you predict who will have to sit down next? How do you know?*

■ The last child standing is the winner.

COUNTING IN MULTIPLES OF 2s, 5s AND 10s

EXTEND

Children practise counting on and back in 10s from any number (for example 5, 13). The child holding the beanbag when 100 is reached must sit down.

10s RACE

You need: a counting stick; number cards (multiples of 10–100 per pair)

STEPS

■ Use the counting stick to practise counting on and back in multiples of 10.

■ Now ask children to count in 10s in their heads as you point to each division on the counting stick. Point to different divisions. Ask: *If we counted from 0 to 100 in 10s, which number do you think this would be? How do you know? What would it look like?*

■ Spread a set of number cards face up on the floor. As a class, order the multiples of 10 from smallest to largest. Notice the pattern of 1, 2, 3, 4 within the numbers. Ask: *What do you notice about all the multiples of 10?* (they end in 0) *What does the first digit in each number tell us about the number?*

■ Give each pair number cards to play a '10s race'. Children shuffle the cards and spread them face down. They race to be the first pair to turn over all their cards and order them from 10 to 100.

■ Play several times, mixing up the pairs.

EXTEND

Use the number cards to play a 'show me' game, for example *Show me the multiple of 10 that is 7 lots of 10. Show me the multiple of 10 that comes before 90.*
Play a '5s race' or '2s race' using multiples of 5 and 2. Children count around the circle in 1s. Anyone who has to say a multiple of 10 must sit down.

PENDULUM COUNT

PAGES 8 TO 9

You need: a pendulum (a small weight tied to a piece of string); number cards (0–50)

STEPS

■ Gently swing the pendulum to set up a counting rhythm.

■ Count in unison in steps of 5 to 50 in time with the pendulum. Then start at 50 and count back in 5s.

■ Repeat several times. Practise counting on and back from different multiples of 5. Then count beyond 50 if appropriate. Vary the speed of the pendulum swings by lengthening or shortening the string. How quickly can children count?

■ Now ask children to count in their heads. What number have they reached when the pendulum stops?

EXTEND

Children count beyond 50. They practise counting in steps of 2 or 10. Using number cards they order multiples of 5 to 50.

COUNTING PATTERNS

You need: digital file (100 square); resource 2 (100 square); coloured pencils; red and blue counters

STEPS

■ Children count on the 100 square (resource 2) in jumps of 5 to 50. They shade in all the numbers they land on. Ask them to look closely at the shaded squares and describe the pattern. Ask: *What do you notice about the shaded numbers? What do we call these numbers?* (multiples of 5) *Can you describe the pattern the multiples of 5 make on the 100 square? What is the same about all of the numbers in the first column? How about the numbers in the second column?*

■ Children then shade the remaining multiples of 5 on their 100 square as quickly as they can, using their knowledge of multiples of 5.

■ Children can use their shaded 100 square to practise counting forwards and backwards in 5s, starting from a different shaded square each time.

EXTEND

Can children continue the count beyond 100? What would the next 5 numbers be? Ask them to explain how they know this. Let them investigate the pattern of 2s and 10s on a 100 square.

MULTIPLES STAIRCASE

You need: multi-link cubes or similar

STEPS

■ Explain that children are going to build a staircase using cubes to show counting in 2s.

■ Discuss the features of an actual staircase and ask children to reflect on what their multiple staircases might look like. Share ideas but allow children to explore further once in their groups.

■ Children work together to build a staircase. Listen carefully to them exploring how to tackle the problem, for example using different coloured cubes for each stair, organising the cubes vertically or horizontally, in squares or towers. Encourage children to explain their thinking or modelling where necessary.

■ Ask groups to share their staircase, explaining their design as well as which multiple each stair represents.

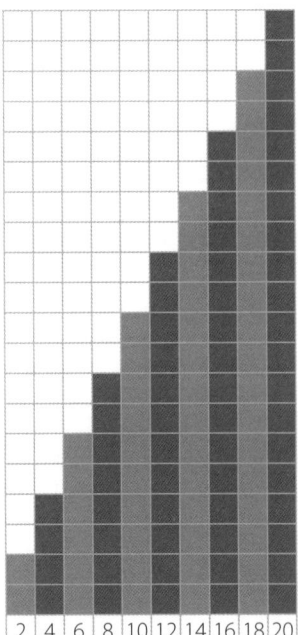

EXTEND

Once children have shared their versions of a staircase, ask them to consider how each staircase was effective. They then draw a multiple staircase using grid paper and label each stair.

WASHING LINE MULTIPLES

You need: for each group a washing line; minimum of 20 clothes pegs; number cards (1–20)

STEPS

■ Explain that children need to hang all the multiples of 2 up to 20 on the washing line.

■ In small groups, ask children to consider how they could organise the numbers on the line to make sure they include all the multiples. Children will likely suggest ordering them from smallest to largest however some may suggest from largest to smallest. Allow children to experiment with how best to organise their washing line numbers rather than telling them; this exploration will reinforce the importance of working systematically.

■ Gather the class together. Encourage reflection with questioning such as: *How did you decide to organise your number line? Why did you not put 0 on your number line? Can you see a pattern? How would you describe it? If I gave you numbers beyond 20 to put on the line, what numbers would you put next? How did you know you had found all the multiples of 2 up to 20?*

EXTEND

Let children think about multiples of 2 beyond 20. If all children organised their multiples in ascending order, ask them to repeat placing them in descending order. Watch to see if they start the task from the beginning or realise that they simply need to swap their positions. This activity works well with other multiples. You could also ask children to work with 2 washing lines, each with different multiples to find common multiples.

WHAT'S WRONG?

You need: digital file 1 (Number sequences)

STEPS

■ Display the first number sequence from digital file 1 (Number sequences) on the board (44 46 48 50 54 56 58 60 64 66 68 72). Explain that some of the numbers are missing.

■ Give children a few minutes to study the number sequence. Ask: *What do you notice about the numbers? Can you see a pattern? Describe the number pattern you can see. Write the missing numbers on your whiteboard.* (52, 62, 70) *Explain how you know that these are the missing numbers.* Show the completed number sequence on screen 2.

■ Repeat for the other missing number sequences.

EXTEND

Create other missing number sequences for children to solve independently.

WHAT'S MY NUMBER?

You need: digital file 2 (What's my number?); a variety of resources (for example number lines, 100 squares, multi-link cubes or similar); coins

STEPS

■ Display digital file 2 (What's my number?) and read the question together (I am thinking of a number that is a multiple of 2, 5 and 10. What could my number be?). Highlight the word multiple and discuss what it means. Explain that you would like children to work in pairs to find examples of numbers that are multiples of 2, 5 and 10.

■ Observe children as they work and ask targeted questions to support and extend their learning. Ask: *Which number are you going to investigate first? Why have you chosen this number? How could you use this apparatus to investigate if the number you have chosen is a multiple of 2, 5 or 10? Can you show me how you could use cubes to investigate whether 20 is a multiple of 2, 5 and 10? Would this be an efficient way to investigate if 99 is a multiple of 2, 5 and 10? What could you use instead of cubes?* (coins, annotating a 100 square)

■ Gather children together, re-read the question and invite them to suggest possible answers. Can they demonstrate the strategy they used? Record correct answers on the board. Say: *Look carefully at the numbers. Do you notice a pattern?* (all the numbers are multiples of 10) *Does this mean a multiple of 10 will always be a multiple of 2 and 5?*

EXTEND

Ask: *Can you tell me a 3-digit number that is a multiple of 2, 5 and 10? How can you be sure you are correct? Is 456 a multiple of 2, 5 and 10? Explain how you know.*

MULTIPLES OF 2 AND 5: WHAT'S THE SAME? WHAT'S DIFFERENT?

You need: 2 large hoops; number cards (1–100)

STEPS

■ Ask each group to set up their hoops as a Venn diagram. Review sorting using Venn diagrams if necessary.

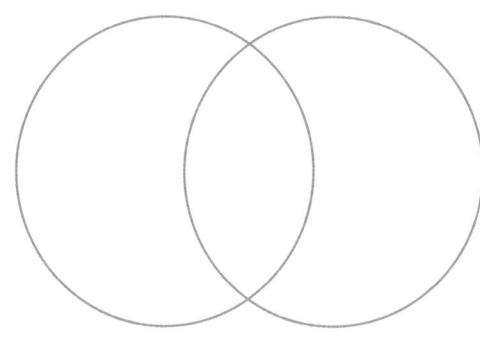

■ Children sort the number cards into the appropriate section of the Venn diagram according to whether they are a multiple of 2 or 5 or both 2 and 5.

■ Ask children to look carefully at the numbers in each section. Ask: *Can you see any patterns?* (for example all are even multiples of 5, or multiples ending in 0) *What do you notice about all the multiples of 5 that are not also multiples of 2?*

EXTEND

Ask children to think about multiples of 2 and 5 beyond 100. Do they think that the pattern will continue? Ask them to explain their reasoning.

COUNTING COLLISION

You need: digital file 3 (Counting collision); a variety of resources (for example number lines, 100 squares, multi-link cubes or similar, or number plates)

STEPS

■ Display the problem from digital file 3 (Counting collision) and read the first part together: *If Sam counts in 2s and Zan counts in 5s, when will they both reach the same number?* Discuss what children have to find out.

■ Encourage children to choose equipment either to find the answer or check that it is correct.

■ As they work, ask questions to assess their understanding, for example: *How did you find your answer? How do you know that you are correct? If Sam and Zan counted backwards from 20 do you know what number they would meet on? What if they counted on from 30? If Sam and Zan counted backwards from 20, when will they reach the same number?*

■ On a 100 square, work together to shade all the multiples of 2 and 5 to 50 that are the same. Encourage children to look for patterns. Ask: *What do you notice about the numbers Sam and Zan meet on?* (they are always a multiple of 10)

EXTEND

Ask: *If Sam and Zan start counting in 2s and 5s from 3, when will they both reach the same number?* (13)

CHANGING PLACES

You need: large number cards (multiples of 2, 5, and 10, 1 card per child)

STEPS

■ Choose a child to stand in the centre.

■ Give everyone sitting in the circle a number card. Ask them to place the card face up on the floor in front of them.

■ Call out an instruction to the child in the middle, for example *Change places with the number that is missing in this sequence: 2, 4, blank, 8. Change places with a number that is a multiple of 5.*

■ Continue the game following instructions of varying difficulty, for example *Change places with the number that comes next in this sequence: 50, 40, 30. Change places with a multiple of 2 that is less than 10. Change places with a number that is a multiple of both 5 and 10.*

■ During the activity ask questions to check children's understanding. Ask: *Why have you chosen to swap places with that number? Can you explain how you know the number you have chosen is a multiple of 2? Can you describe the number sequence in your own words?*

EXTEND

Give instructions that require several members of the group to get up and change places at the same time, for example *Multiples of 5, all change!*

DOUBLING

Recognising and recalling doubles of whole numbers is an early multiplication skill. Using the correct vocabulary, doubling can be introduced practically using everyday objects and pictures, such as counting the spots on dominoes or ladybirds. Many children may already have experience from playing dice games and dominoes.

Children should have opportunities to learn and develop quick recall of doubling facts for numbers to 12. They should be taught to choose and use suitable strategies for doubling larger numbers when playing games or solving simple everyday problems such as while shopping or baking (for example how to partition a 2-digit number into 10s and 1s before doubling it). Mastery of doubling can support children's developing understanding of early multiplication in several ways, for example understanding that doubling can be shown as repeated addition using the symbols + and = (3 + 3 = 6) or multiplying a number by 2 (3 × 2 = 6). In these activities, children are shown how to partition a 2-digit number into 10s and 1s and how to recognise odd and even numbers.

I rolled 2 5s. That's double 5! That's 10 altogether.

Activity	Objective	Focus	Organisation	Development
Body doubles! (p18)	Solve 1-step problems involving multiplication and division, using materials, arrays, repeated addition, mental methods, and multiplication and division facts, including problems in context	Using concrete resources to introduce the concept of doubling	Whole class	Fluency
Tower blocks (p18)		Using concrete resources to provide a visual sense of calculating doubles	Pairs	Problem-solving
Ladybird doubles (p19)		Using pictorial resources to practise doubling small quantities. Recording a double as a number sentence using the symbols + and =	Whole class/ pairs	Fluency and reasoning
Domino doubles (p19)	Solve 1-step problems involving multiplication and division	Using concrete resources to get a visual sense of calculating doubles. To record a double as a number sentence using the symbols + and =	Whole class	Fluency
Shopping spree (p20)	Solve problems involving multiplication and division, using materials, arrays, repeated addition, mental methods, and multiplication and division facts, including problems in contexts (Year 2)	Learning how to double a 2-digit number by partitioning	Whole class/ individuals	Problem-solving
Magic bean (p20)		Doubling a 2-digit number by partitioning	Whole class/ small groups	Problem-solving and reasoning
Fairy cakes (p21)		Selecting suitable strategies to double numbers	Individuals/ pairs	Fluency

Activity	Objective	Focus	Organisation	Development
Playing cards (p21)	Recall and use multiplication and division facts for the 2-, 5-, and 10-multiplication tables, including recognising odd and even numbers (Year 2)	Developing quick recall of known doubles facts	Whole class	Fluency
Hot potato (p21)		Developing quick recall of known doubles	Whole class standing in a circle	Fluency
Double it! (p21)		Developing quick recall of doubles facts for multiples of 5 and 10	Pairs	Fluency

Assessing progress

Use these questions (or similar) to help you assess children's understanding during and after these activities.

- Show children 2 dominoes (for example 3 spots/3 spots and 4 spots/5 spots). *Which domino is a double?* *How do you know?*

- *Can you roll a double with 2 dice? How do you know it is a double?*

- *Can you draw spots on a domino to show double 5?*

- *What is double 5? Double 12? Double 20?*

- *There are 6 apples in a bag. How many apples in 2 bags?*

- *If half of 12 is 6, what is double 6?*

BODY DOUBLES!

You need: no resources required

STEPS

■ Pick a child to stand at the front. Ask the class: *How many legs on this body? How many arms? How many fingers?* and so on.

■ Invite a second child to the front. Pose the same questions. Encourage children to explain how the answers have changed. Model and discuss appropriate language (for example greater, bigger, twice as many, double).

■ Practise calculating doubles of small numbers. Everyone holds up 7 fingers, finds a partner and holds up their fingers side by side to show double 7. Invite 1 pair to describe what their fingers show. (double 7 makes 14) Practise doubling other numbers in this way.

EXTEND

Ask children to represent a double using apparatus and to draw a picture that shows a double.

TOWER BLOCKS

You need: multi-link cubes or similar

STEPS

■ Hold up a tower of 4 cubes. Challenge children to build a tower which is double its height.

■ Look at the children's towers. Discuss: *Are the towers taller or shorter than my tower? How much taller?* Choose a child who has answered correctly to describe in their own words how they approached the problem and checked their answer.

■ Repeat with cube towers of different heights. Ask children to represent their answer pictorially or using symbols (for example drawing blocks, annotating a number line, as an addition sentence).

EXTEND

Children investigate halving small numbers. Ask: *Can you build a tower that is half the height of this tower?*

LADYBIRD DOUBLES

PAGES 12 TO 13

You need: digital file 4 (Ladybird doubles); whiteboards and pens; counters; cubes; number lines

STEPS

■ Show children digital file 4 (Ladybird doubles) and look at the ladybird picture. Ask: *How many spots does the ladybird have on each wing? How many spots altogether? Let's say together, "double 4 makes 8".*

■ Ask children to represent the double as a number sentence: 4 + 4 = 8.

■ Draw the outline of a ladybird on the board. Draw an equal number of spots on each wing. Ask: *What can you tell me about the spots on this ladybird? Is it a double? Why?* (there is an equal/the same number of spots) *How could we represent the number of spots as an addition sentence?*

■ Repeat, this time drawing an unequal number of spots. Ask: *Is this ladybird a double? Why not?*

■ In pairs, children imagine a ladybird with 16 spots. Can you work out how many spots the ladybird has on each wing? Encourage children to calculate, check and explain the problem using practical apparatus (for example fingers, cubes, number track), pictures and/or symbols. Ask: *How did you work out the answer?*

EXTEND

Using cubes or playing cards, children work out the doubles of larger numbers. They investigate halving small numbers for example *I am imagining a ladybird. It has 10 spots altogether. How many spots are on each wing?*

DOMINO DOUBLES

You need: a small bag containing all the domino doubles; 1 whiteboard and pen per child

STEPS

■ Choose a volunteer to take a domino out of the bag without showing it to the other children.

■ Ask them to say which domino it is (for example double 5). Tell children to draw a picture of what they think the domino looks like. Show them the double 5 domino. Ask: *Does the domino you have drawn look like this? How did you know how many spots to draw on each side of the domino?* Count how many spots are on the domino altogether. Say together, *Double 5 makes 10*. Return the domino to the bag.

■ Repeat several times with different children picking a domino out of the bag.

■ Ask children to draw all the doubles in a set of dominoes and write a number sentence to describe each double.

EXTEND

Children practise quick recall of doubles facts from 0–6. Call out a double, for example *Double 6!* Children shout out the correct answer as quickly as they can.

SHOPPING SPREE

You need: coins (10p, 1p); 4 items each labelled with a price tag: 14p, 22p, 43p, 31p

STEPS

■ Hold up an item and read out the price, for example a teddy priced at 14p.

■ Tell children that you would like to know how much it would cost to buy 2 teddies. *What do you need to do to the price?* (double it) Ask children to suggest different strategies they might use to calculate double 14 (for example using concrete apparatus, counting on, using their knowledge of 10s and 1s).

■ Demonstrate how to double a 2-digit number by partitioning. First, partition 14 into 10s and 1s and then double each part. This can be shown visually using coins. Add the totals together to get double 14.

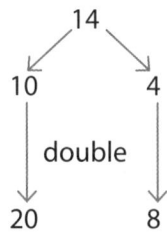

■ Work together to double the price of the other items by partitioning.

■ Write a list of prices on the board. Working individually, ask children to double each price by partitioning.

EXTEND

Children use partitioning to double the cost of higher priced items (for example £1.32). Adapt the activity to practise halving numbers. *What would the price of a different collection of items be in a half-price sale?*

MAGIC BEAN

You need: digital file 5 (Magic bean); cubes; rulers; base 10; 100 squares; whiteboards and pens

STEPS

■ Display digital file 5 (Magic bean) and read the problem together: *Jack plants a magic bean in his garden. It grows into a great beanstalk. After 1 week the beanstalk is 12m tall. The beanstalk doubles in height each week. How tall will the beanstalk be after 3 weeks?*). Ask: *What is the problem asking us to find out? What do we know already?*

■ Using equipment of their choice, give children time to work out the height of the beanstalk at week 2 and week 3. (Quick finishers can also try to work out the height of the beanstalk at weeks 4 and 5.) Ask children to explain their method to their group.

■ Evaluate children's strategies (for example partitioning, practical apparatus, counting on a 100 square). Ask them to consider which methods might be most efficient to use when working with larger numbers and why.

■ Ask children to use partitioning to solve the second problem: *Jack plants another magic bean in his garden. It grows into a great beanstalk. After 1 week the beanstalk is 23m tall. The beanstalk doubles in height each week. How tall will the beanstalk be after 3 weeks?*

EXTEND

Ask: *Can you work out the height of the beanstalk after 5 weeks?* Children could investigate how to use partitioning to double 3-digit numbers.

FAIRY CAKES

You need: resource 3 (Fairy cakes)

STEPS

■ Give each child a copy of resource 3 (Fairy cakes). Ask them to double the recipe to give the quantities of each ingredient needed to make 24 fairy cakes.

■ Observe children as they complete the task. Talk to them about what they are doing. If necessary, remind them of strategies they could use to double larger numbers for example counting on in jumps of 10 and 1 from a number on a 100 square or number track, or by partitioning (see previous activities in this section).

■ Quick finishers could try to double the recipe again to work out the amount of each ingredient required to make 48 cakes.

EXTEND

Let children double quantities for other recipes or double the weights/capacities of a selection of tins, packets and bottles.

PLAYING CARDS

You need: a shuffled pack of giant playing cards (with numbers covered)

STEPS

■ Divide the class into 2 teams. Choose 1 child from each team to stand up.

■ Turn over the top card of the pack. The first child to double the number on the card correctly scores a point for their team.

■ Repeat, choosing different children to stand up, until all of the cards have been used.

■ The team with the most points at the end of the game is the winner.

EXTEND

Children play the game using different sets of numbers (for example multiples of 5 or 10). Children play with a time limit. *Double the number on as many cards as you can within the time. Play again. Can you beat your previous score?*

HOT POTATO

You need: a beanbag

STEPS

■ Say that the beanbag is a hot potato. Explain that the potato is so hot that you won't want to hold it for any more than a few seconds.

■ Stand in the middle of the circle and throw the hot potato to someone, calling out *Double 10!* Whoever catches the hot potato must throw it back, calling out the answer at the same time.

■ Throw the hot potato to different children, calling out a different double each time. Children should answer as quickly as possible so that the hot potato doesn't get too hot in their hands.

EXTEND

Turn the activity into a competitive game. If children answer incorrectly or take a long time to throw the beanbag back, they must sit down. The last few children standing are the winners.

DOUBLE IT!

You need: resource 4 (Double it!); counters in 2 colours; number cards (multiples of 5–50)

STEPS

■ Give pairs a copy of resource 4 (Double it!). Children take turns to play. Player 1 turns over a card, doubles the number and covers the total on the game board with a counter. Player 2 checks the answer to make sure it is correct.

■ If a player makes, for example 30, and all the 30s on the board have already been covered, they miss a turn. When all the cards have been turned over, they shuffle the cards and continue.

■ Question children while they are playing to develop understanding. Ask: *Where would you like to put your next counter? What card do you need to turn over to allow you to cover the number 60, 80 etc? Explain why. How could you use partitioning to help you double 35?*

■ The winner is the child with the most counters on the board when the time is up.

EXTEND

The game board can easily be adapted to practise multiplication facts for other doubles.

3 EQUAL GROUPS

During the early stages of learning about multiplication and division, it is essential that children develop a secure understanding of equal grouping and sharing. This understanding includes being able to reason about odd and even numbers, a Year 2 objective. Children should be taught to recognise, make and describe equal groups using a variety of concrete objects and pictorial representations. It is important to familiarise children with appropriate mathematical vocabulary, for example equal groups, unequal groups, lots of and so on.

There are 4 carrots on each plate. There are 4 carrots in each group.
There is an equal/the same number of carrots on each plate/in each group.
There are 12 carrots altogether.

Activity	Objective	Focus	Organisation	Development
Snack time (p23)		Recognising, making and describing equal groupings using concrete objects	Whole class sitting in a circle/pairs	Fluency
Sorting sheep (p23)		Recognising equal and unequal groupings and practising making equal sets using pictorial resources	Small groups	Problem-solving and reasoning
Odd 1 out (p24)	Solve 1-step problems involving multiplication and division by calculating the answer using concrete objects, pictorial representations and arrays with the support of the teacher	Developing children's understanding of and ability to describe, make and reason about equal groupings using visual resources	Whole class/ small groups	Reasoning and problem-solving
Am I right? (p24)		Investigating whether it is always possible to arrange an even number of objects into equal groups and reason about odd and even numbers to 20	Pairs	Problem-solving and reasoning
Grabbing game (p24)		Sorting concrete objects into equal groups	Pairs	Problem-solving

Assessing progress

Use these questions (or similar) to help you assess children's understanding during and after these activities.

- Draw children an image of groups (for example 3 goldfish bowls with 4 goldfish in each bowl). *Are these groups equal? How do you know?*

- *Arrange 12 cubes into equal groups. How many groups? How many cubes in each group?*

- *How many different ways can you group 14 counters?*

- *How many pairs can you make from 20 shoes?*

- *Can you arrange 7 beads into 2 equal groups? Why not?*

SNACK TIME

PAGES 14 TO 15

You need: 12 biscuits (real or pretend); paper plates; cubes; whiteboards and pens

STEPS

■ Set out 3 paper plates and place 4 biscuits on each plate. Ask children to describe in their own words how the biscuits have been grouped. Encourage them to use mathematical language such as: same, equal, groups.

■ Write on the board: *There are _ equal groups with _ biscuits within each group.* Together, fill in the missing numbers and then read the sentence. Ask: *What does the 3 or 4 represent?*

■ Set up the activity again, this time with 5 plates and 2 biscuits on each plate, encouraging children to describe equal groups using appropriate mathematical vocabulary.

■ With children in pairs, give each pair some paper plates and some cubes to represent biscuits. Set some simple problems for children to solve practically, for example *Imagine you have 12 biscuits. Arrange the biscuits on 3 plates so that there is an equal number of biscuits on each plate. Describe the equal groups you have made.*

EXTEND

Repeat this activity in a variety of contexts to develop children's ability to recognise, describe and make equal groups, for example candles on cakes, coins in purses, flowers in vases.

SORTING SHEEP

You need: digital file 6 (Sorting sheep); resource 5 (Sorting sheep); scissors; number cards (1–12) for each group

STEPS

■ Display the first screen of digital file 6 (Sorting sheep). Say: *Look at how the farmer has grouped his sheep. Are the groups equal? How many groups of sheep are there? How many sheep are in each group?*

■ Display the second screen. Say: *Look at how the farmer has sorted his sheep now. How many groups of sheep are there? Are the groups equal? What could he do to make the groups equal?* (move a sheep across/add 2 more sheep/take 2 sheep away)

■ Give each group a copy of resource 5 (Sorting sheep). Children cut out the sheep cards and turn over a number card. Tell them that they must pretend to be a farmer, so if they turn over card number 9, they put 9 sheep in their fields. They should try to arrange the sheep so there is an equal number in each field. Note: they don't have to use all the fields.

■ They repeat until all the number cards have been turned over.

■ Question children to assess understanding. Ask: *How many groups of sheep? How many sheep in each group? You have sorted 12 sheep into 2 equal sets. Now investigate if you can sort 12 sheep into 3 sets. Have you found any numbers you can't split into equal groups?*

EXTEND

Children investigate how many ways they can sort 8 sheep into equal groups (8 groups of 1, 4 groups of 2, 2 groups of 4, 1 group of 8). Ask them to draw pictures to record their findings.

ODD 1 OUT

You need: digital file 7 (Odd 1 out)

STEPS

■ Display digital file 7 (Odd 1 out) and look at the images. Children tell their neighbour which they think is the odd 1 out and why.

■ Share ideas. Can children correctly identify the odd 1 out? (the set of dice) Ask: *Why don't the dice belong in this set?* (the dice represent 4 equal groups of 5 but all the other images show 3 equal groups of 5) *What could we do to the dice to make them belong?* (cross 1 out)

■ Ask: *Can you think of a different way of showing 3 equal groups of 5? How could I draw a picture of this grouping?*

■ Ask children to think of other ways of representing 3 equal groups of 5 and to draw pictures to record their ideas.

EXTEND

Children make an 'odd 1 out' puzzle for a partner to solve.

AM I RIGHT?

You need: digital file 8 (Am I right?); small counting apparatus (cubes, counters, buttons)

STEPS

■ Spend a few minutes revising even and odd numbers. Say: *Look at the class number line. Which numbers are even? Which numbers are odd?*

■ Display the word problem from digital file 8 (Am I right?) and read it together.

■ Children investigate the problem and draw pictures to show what they find out.

■ Discuss what children have found out. Ask them to share their examples to prove that an even number can always be shared into 2 equal groups. *Can you explain why?*

■ Ask: *What do you think would happen if you tried to divide an odd number into 2 equal groups? Why do you think this? Work with your partner to see if you are right.*

EXTEND

Children investigate how many different ways they can sort 20 cubes into equal groups.

GRABBING GAME

You need: trays containing up to 50 small objects (cubes, counters, coins, dried beans or pasta shapes)

STEPS

■ Demonstrate the game. Ask a volunteer to grab a big handful of objects from the tray. Ask them to try and divide the objects into equal groups. If they can do this they will score a point.

■ Give each pair a tray of objects and paper and pencil to keep score.

■ Children take turns to play. Discuss with them what they are doing. Do they understand that there may be a different way of sorting the objects into equal groups if their first attempt is unsuccessful? Ask targeted questions to assess and extend their learning: *How many beans are in each group? How many groups?*

■ Link to previous activity, Am I right? Say: *Count the objects you have grabbed. Do you think you will be able to arrange this number of objects into equal groups? Why? Would you rather grab an even number of objects or an odd number? Why?* (an even number can always be arranged into 2 or more even groups; some odd numbers cannot be made into equal groups)

■ The child with the most points after 10 turns each is the winner.

EXTEND

Let children investigate: *Which of the odd numbers from 1 to 19 can be arranged into equal groups? How can 20 flowers be arranged in vases so that each vase has the same number of flowers?*

ADDING EQUAL GROUPS

Once children are able to recognise and make equal groups of objects using concrete apparatus and pictorial representations, they should be shown how to combine these groups using repeated addition. These activities provide opportunities for children to use repeated addition to solve simple multiplication problems. A range of strategies are introduced: acting out problems with concrete apparatus, drawing pictorial representations and adding equal groups by making jumps on a number line.

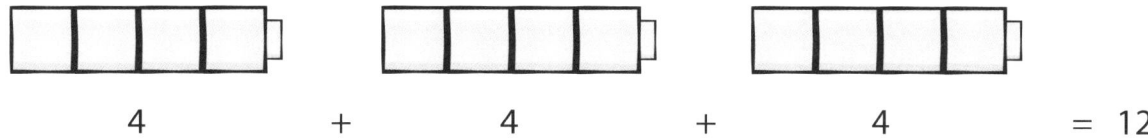

4 + 4 + 4 = 12

Activity	Objective	Focus	Organisation	Development
Winter warmers (p26)	Solve problems involving multiplication and division, using materials, arrays, repeated addition, mental methods, and multiplication and division facts, including problems in contexts (Year 2)	Introducing multiplication as repeated addition	Whole class	Fluency
Bead strings (p26)		Using concrete resources to make equal groups and writing repeated addition sentences relating to the groupings	Whole class/ small groups	Fluency
Farmyard stories (p26)		Making equal groups and writing repeated addition sentences relating to the groupings	Whole class/ pairs	Reasoning, fluency
Roll it! (p27)	Making equal groups and writing repeated addition sentences relating to the groupings	Practising adding equal groups	Whole class/ small groups	Fluency
Adding equal groups on a number line (p27)	Solve problems involving multiplication and division, using materials, arrays, repeated addition, mental methods, and multiplication and division facts, including problems in contexts (Year 2)	Exploring addition of equal groups on a number line	Whole class/ small groups	Problem-solving
Would you rather? (p27)		Choosing an appropriate strategy to add equal groups	Whole class/ pairs	Reasoning, problem-solving

Assessing progress

Use these questions (or similar) to help you assess children's understanding during and after these activities.

- *How many gloves in 7 pairs?*
- *How many toes on 5 feet?*
- *If you had 7 10ps in your money box, how much money would you have altogether?*
- *Add 2 + 2 + 2 + 2 using concrete apparatus.*
- *Draw a picture to help you add 3 equal groups of 5.*
- *Can you add 7 groups of 2 on a number line?*

WINTER WARMERS

PAGES 16 TO 17

You need: a basket containing 10 pairs of socks; 20 pegs; a washing line; number and symbol cards (even numbers to 20, 10 '2' cards, 10 '+' cards, 1 '=' card)

STEPS

- Ask a child to take 4 pairs of socks out of the basket and to peg them on the washing line in pairs. Ask: *How many pairs of socks? How many in each pair? How many altogether? Encourage children to count the socks in 2s.*

- Working together, arrange the number and symbol cards to make a calculation to represent how the equal groups were added (2 + 2 + 2 + 2 = 8). Ask: *Why have we used the addition symbol more than once? What does the 8 show? Why have we added 2 4 times?*

- Repeat, changing the number of pairs of socks each time. Choose different children to arrange the number and symbol cards to make a number sentence each time. Alternatively, ask children to record number sentences individually on whiteboards.

EXTEND

Ask: *How many gloves would you need for 7 children to each have a pair to wear? How do you know? How many pairs could I make with 18 socks?*

BEAD STRINGS

You need: digital file 9 (Bead strings); pots of coloured beads and strings; whiteboards and pens

STEPS

- Display the bead string from digital file 9 (Bead strings) on the board. Look at the beads and the number sentence together. Ask: *How are the beads grouped? How many altogether? What is the number sentence describing? What do the 2s represent? What does the 10 mean? Why has the addition symbol been used?*

- Give each group a pot of beads and a string. Ask them to thread 6 equal groups of 2 beads onto the string, remembering to alternate the colours. Ask them to write a number sentence to describe the arrangement of beads.

- Create a list of groupings on the board (for example 7 equal groups of 2, 4 equal groups of 2, 10 equal groups of 2).

- Tell children to make a bead string and write a number sentence to describe each equal grouping.

EXTEND

Children make a bead string to match a number sentence (for example 3 + 3 + 3 + 3 = 12).

FARMYARD STORIES

You need: whiteboards and pens

STEPS

- Tell a farmyard number story, for example A farmer has 4 fields. He puts 2 cows in each field. How many cows does he have altogether?

■ Say that you are going to draw a picture to represent the problem. Ask: *How many fields do I need to draw? How many cows shall I draw in each field?* Count the cows in 2s to find the answer. Record this as a number sentence on the board: 2 + 2 + 2 + 2 = 8.

■ Make up similar problems for children to solve in pairs. Ask them to draw a picture of their number story on their whiteboard and to write a repeated addition to represent it.

EXTEND

Children add sets of 2p, 5p or 10p coins. They show their working as an addition sentence.

ROLL IT!

You need: resource 6 (Roll it!); a blank dice labelled 2, 2, 5, 5, 10, 10; a 1–6 dice; coins (2p, 5p, 10p)

STEPS

■ Explain that children will practise making and adding equal groups.

■ Model how to play the game and explain the dice: the 1–6 dice shows how many equal groups to make and the 2, 5, 10 dice shows how many are in each group. Roll both dice and work together to represent the equal groups with coins, for example if 6 and 10 are rolled, lay out 6 10p coins. Work out the total value of the coins by counting in 10s. Cover the total with a counter on the game board on resource 6 (Roll it!). Repeat several times until everyone understands how to play.

■ Organise children into groups. Explain that whoever has the most counters on the board at the end of the game is the winner.

■ Observe children as they play. Ask targeted questions to support learning and assess understanding: *How many equal groups are there? How are you going to count the total amount of money? What numbers would I need to roll to be able to cover number 25? Explain how you know this.*

EXTEND

Children write addition sentences to describe the equal groups. They play the game without the coins. They roll the dice and count the equal groups mentally.

ADDING EQUAL GROUPS ON A NUMBER LINE

You need: digital file 10 (Adding equal groups on a number line); resource 7 (Adding equal groups); pencils

STEPS

■ Display the word problem from digital file 10 (Adding equal groups on a number line) and read it together: *There are 5 flowers in each vase. How many flowers altogether? Can you show this problem as a repeated addition on the number line?* Discuss what children have to find out.

■ Work together to add the equal groups on the number line. Draw in the jumps and write '+5' above each jump on the number line to reinforce the addition of 4 equal groups of 5.

■ Ask: *How many flowers are there altogether? How do we know? How would this look as a number sentence?*

■ Ask children to solve similar problems by drawing jumps on the number line from resource 7 (Adding equal groups).

EXTEND

Children draw a picture and make up a number story for a given number line.

WOULD YOU RATHER?

You need: digital file 11 (Would you rather?); practical counting apparatus; whiteboards and pens

STEPS

■ Display digital file 11 (Would you rather?) and read the word problem together: *Would you rather have 5 packets with 10 sweets in or 7 packets with 5 sweets in?* Discuss what children have to find out.

■ As children work, listen carefully to them exploring how to tackle the problem (for example using cubes to represent sweets, making equal jumps on a number line, writing out number sentences). Encourage children to explain their working using appropriate mathematical language.

■ Invite different pairs to answer the problem, explaining why they have made this choice. (Remember, either answer could be correct as long as it is supported by a good reason.)

5 ARRAYS

Arrays provide a visual image to repeated addition. They can be used to develop children's understanding of multiplication and to formally introduce multiplication facts. Examples of arrays in everyday life, such as egg boxes, chocolate bars and food packaging are good introductions. Children should be given opportunities to make, draw and interpret arrays using objects such as counters, stickers, pegboards and squared paper. The commutative property of multiplication, normally introduced in Year 2, can be clearly illustrated using an array. For example the array below could be interpreted as 3 rows of 5 or 5 columns of 3. Whichever way you interpret it, there will always be 15 dots.

Activity	Objective	Focus	Organisation	Development
Arrays in many ways (p29)	Solve 1-step problems involving multiplication and division, by calculating the answer using concrete objects, pictorial representations and arrays with the support of the teacher (Year 1)	Using concrete apparatus to make arrays	Whole class/ pairs	Fluency
A spotty problem (p29)		Making an array to find the answer to a simple problem	Pairs	Problem-solving
Everyday arrays (p30)		Developing awareness of the commutative property of multiplication ($6 \times 5 = 5 \times 6$)	Whole class	Fluency, reasoning
Chocolate bar arrays (p30)	Show that multiplication of 2 numbers can be done in any order (commutative) and division of 1 number by another cannot (Year 2)	Making and describing arrays	Individuals	Fluency, reasoning
Roller coaster (p30)	Solve problems involving multiplication and division, using materials, arrays, repeated addition, mental methods, and multiplication and division facts, including problems in contexts (Year 2)	Using knowledge of arrays to solve a multiplication problem	Pairs	Problem-solving
Let's investigate (p31)		Using knowledge of arrays to solve a multiplication problem	Pairs	Problem-solving, reasoning
Sometimes, always or never (p31)		Using knowledge of arrays to reason about numbers	Small groups	Reasoning, problem-solving

Assessing progress

Use these questions (or similar) to help you assess children's understanding during and after these activities.

- *Can you arrange 12 counters into an array? How many rows? How many columns?*
- *Draw an array to show 4 × 5.*
- *Draw an array of 3 rows of 5 counters. Can you write 2 multiplications to describe this array?*
- *How many different arrays can you make with 12 cubes?*

ARRAYS IN MANY WAYS

You need: digital file 12 (Arrays in many ways); pots containing small objects (rubbers, counters, cubes, coins, pompoms, sequins, buttons, acorns, milk bottle tops, dried beans or pasta); a 6 × 6 grid

STEPS

- Display digital file 12 (Arrays in many ways) and ask children to describe the arrangement of dinosaur counters. Ask: *How many rows of counters? How many counters are in each row? How many altogether? How do you know? Did anyone count the dinosaurs in a group? Why?* (I know how to count on in steps of 5. It is quicker than counting in 1s.)

- Explain that when objects or pictures are arranged into columns and rows, as the dinosaurs are, we call it an array. Demonstrate how to make an array on a blank grid (for example 2 rows of 3 buttons). Talk about the array that has been created. Ask: *How many rows of buttons? How many buttons in each row? How many altogether?*

- In pairs, children take turns to make different arrays on a blank grid. They describe each array to their partner, using a different set of objects each time.

EXTEND

Children practise making and describing larger arrays. They use playing cards (without pictures) and split the cards into 2 piles. They turn over the top card on each pile to determine the number of the rows and columns in the array.

A SPOTTY PROBLEM

You need: digital file 13 (A spotty problem); counters

STEPS

- Explain that children are going to demonstrate how to make an array to solve a simple multiplication problem.

- Display the problem in digital file 13 (A spotty problem) and read it aloud: *There are 4 aliens. Each alien has 5 spots. How many spots are there altogether?* Demonstrate how to use an array to solve the problem. Ask: *How many spots does the first alien have?* (5) Arrange 5 counters in a row to represent the spots. *How many spots does the second alien have?* (5) Place 5 counters in a row under the first row. Continue until each alien's spots have been represented by counters.

- Talk about the array. Ask: *What does each counter represent?* (a spot) *Why are there 4 rows of counters?* (there are 4 aliens) *Why are there 5 counters in each row?* (each alien has 5 spots)

- Demonstrate how to count in 5s to find out how many spots the 4 aliens have altogether. Ask: *Could I have counted the spots in a different way?* (in 1s or 4s) *Why do you think I counted in 5s?* (We know how to count on in steps of 5. It is quicker than counting in 1s.)

- In pairs, children use counters to make arrays to find the answer to other spotty problems, for example *There are 7 aliens. Each alien has 2 spots. How many spots altogether? Describe the array you have created. What does it show?*

EXTEND

Children make up a spotty problem for their partner who writes the corresponding multiplication next to each array created.

EVERYDAY ARRAYS

You need: a bag with a variety of everyday items that show arrays (for example muffin tins, different sized egg boxes, different sized building bricks, seed trays); whiteboards and pens; a stick of base 10; a peg board with pegs showing an array

STEPS

■ Talk about arrays. Ask: *What is an array? What do you know about each row or column in an array? How can an array help us count a set of objects more efficiently?*

■ Talk about everyday arrays. Ask children to think of examples of arrays they might see in everyday places, for example at home, in the classroom or at the supermarket.

■ Choose a volunteer to take an item out of the bag (for example a 3 × 4 muffin tin). Ask: *Can you describe the array? How many rows?* (3) *How many holes in each row?* (4) *How many holes altogether?* (12) In pairs, children write a repeated addition to describe the array: 4 + 4 + 4 = 12.

■ Pass the muffin tin to other children. *Can anyone think of a different way to describe the array?* (4 rows of 3 holes) *Record this as a repeated addition on your whiteboard.* (3 + 3 + 3 + 3 = 12)

■ Look at the 2 calculations. Ask: *What do you notice?* (3 lots of 4 is the same as 4 lots of 3)

■ Repeat for other objects in the bag.

EXTEND

Ask children to draw an array to show for example 4 + 4 + 4 + 4 + 4 = 5 + 5 + 5 + 5.

CHOCOLATE BAR ARRAYS

You need: digital file 14 (Chocolate bar arrays); cubes; sheets of squared paper; coloured crayons

STEPS

■ Display digital file 14 (Chocolate bar arrays) and look at the chocolate bar image. Ask children to use mathematical language to describe the array. Count how many rows of chocolate and how many pieces of chocolate are in each row.

■ Give a child 10 cubes and ask them to arrange them to represent the chocolate bar.

■ Demonstrate how to record the array by colouring in the correct arrangement of squares on a piece of squared paper. Ask: *How many pieces of chocolate altogether? What are the 2 ways we can write this array as a multiplication?* (2 × 5 = 10 and 5 × 2 = 10)

■ Let children explore making chocolate bar arrays with different numbers of cubes. Give each child some cubes, a sheet of squared paper and a crayon. Ask them to record each chocolate bar array they make and write 2 multiplications to describe the pattern.

EXTEND

Children investigate how many different shaped chocolate bar arrays they could make with, for example 18 cubes.

ROLLER COASTER

You need: digital file 15 (Roller coaster); 36 counters or cubes per pair

STEPS

■ Display digital file 15 (Roller coaster) and read the first part of the problem together: *36 children are queuing to go on the roller coaster. The roller coaster has 3 carriages. Each carriage has 4 rows of 2 seats. How many children will not be able to get a seat on the roller coaster?* Check that children have understood what they have to do. Explain that you would like them to model the problem with apparatus and then draw arrays to demonstrate the answer.

■ Give children time to work out the answer. Listen carefully to them exploring how to tackle the problem; provide support if necessary.

■ Gather children together, re-read the question and ask each pair to feedback their answer. (12 children wouldn't get a seat on the roller coaster) Ask different pairs to demonstrate how they worked out the total number of seats and to explain how they used this information to calculate the answer.

■ Read the second part of the problem together. Challenge pairs to design a roller coaster that would fit all 36 children at the same time.

■ Ask pairs to share their roller coaster, explaining

their design. Recognise that there is more than 1 correct answer.

EXTEND

Pairs that finish quickly could investigate different solutions or design a roller coaster for a different number of people.

LET'S INVESTIGATE

You need: digital file 16 (Let's investigate); counters

STEPS

■ Ask: *What is an array? How can we use arrays to help us solve mathematical problems? Can you arrange 18 counters into an array? Can you describe the array you have made to the person sitting next to you? Do all of the arrays look the same? Why not?*

■ Display digital file 16 (Let's investigate) and read the word problem together: *How many different arrays can you make with 12 counters?* Encourage children to describe in their own words what they need to do.

■ Children investigate how many different arrays they can make with 12 counters. Observe how they tackle the problem and record ideas, offering support where necessary. Ask: *How are you going to remember all the different arrays you make?* (for example draw the arrays, write number sentences) *If you know 1 × 12 = 12, what else do you know? How do you know you have found all the possible arrays?*

■ As a class, re-read the word problem and discuss what children have found out. Ask: *How many different arrays were you able to make?* (6) *How do you know you have found all of the arrays? Can you describe each array?* (1 × 12; 12 × 1; 2 × 6; 6 × 2; 3 × 4; 4 × 3) *How did you record the arrays?*

EXTEND

Children repeat the investigation with a different numbers of counters.

SOMETIMES, ALWAYS OR NEVER

You need: digital file 17 (Sometimes, always, never); cubes; counters; coins; squared paper

STEPS

■ Display digital file 17 (Sometimes, always, never) and read the problem through together: *An even number of objects can be made into more than 1 array and an odd number of objects can only be made into a 1-row array.*

■ Write on the board: *What is an array? What does a 1-row array look like? What do you need to find out? How could you investigate whether the statements are correct? What apparatus could you use? How could you record your findings?* Give children a few minutes to discuss ideas in small groups.

■ Observe children as they work. Ask them what they are doing and offer support if necessary. Ask: *Can you show me how you could use cubes to investigate whether 18 cubes can be arranged into more than 1 array?*

■ Gather the class together. Re-read the first statement: *An even number of objects can be made into more than 1 array* and ask each group to state whether they think it is true sometimes, always or never. Can they explain how they came to this conclusion and show evidence they have collected to demonstrate this? (The first statement is sometimes true. With the exception of 2, all even numbers can be made into more than 1 array.)

■ Re-read the second statement: *An odd number of objects can only be made into a 1-row array.* Do children think this is true sometimes, always or never? (This statement is also sometimes true.) Ask children to look at their results and give examples of odd numbers that can only be made into 1-row arrays (for example 7, 13) and those which can be made into more than 1 array (for example 15, 9).

■ Can children reason why even numbers can always be made into 2-row arrays but odd numbers cannot? (there is always 1 left over)

EXTEND

Children investigate which numbers from 0–30 can be made into square arrays. (4, 15, 25)

6

THE MULTIPLICATION SIGN

These activities provide suggestions for teaching children to read, write and interpret mathematical statements involving multiplication using the multiplication (×) and equals (=) signs. The activities provide opportunities for children to develop their understanding of and ability to use a variety of language to describe multiplication, for example 'lots of', 'times', 'multiplied by'. Using concrete and pictorial resources to represent equal groups, the activities build on children's understanding of grouping and repeated addition. Throughout this book the multiplication sign (×) is described as 'lots of' or 'groups of' rather than the more mathematical 'multiplied by' which reverses the repeated addition (for example 3 × 5 is expressed as 3 *lots of* 5 (5 + 5 + 5) rather than 3 *multiplied by* 5 (3 + 3 + 3 + 3 + 3). This approach has been taken to provide continuity throughout the activities in the book.

Activity	Objective	Focus	Organisation	Development
Introducing the multiplication sign (p33)	Calculate mathematical statements for multiplication and division within the multiplication tables and write them using the multiplication (×), division (÷) and equals (=) signs (Year 2)	Introducing the multiplication sign (×) and associated vocabulary	Whole class/ small groups	Fluency
Complete the table (p33)		Developing understanding of the links between grouping, repeated addition and multiplication	Individuals	Fluency
Tell me a story (p34)		Identifying the correct multiplication sentence to describe a number story	Whole class in pairs	Reasoning, problem-solving
Getting ready for winter (p34)	Solve problems involving multiplication and division, using materials, arrays, repeated addition, mental methods, and multiplication and division facts, including problems in contexts (Year 2)	Using concrete apparatus to act out a multiplication problem and writing multiplication sentences using the multiplication (×) and equals signs (=)	Pairs	Problem-solving
Am I right? (p34)		Relating multiplication to repeated addition and practising writing number sentences using the multiplication (×) sign	Whole class/ small groups	Reasoning, problem-solving
If this is the answer, what is the question? (p35)		Investigating which numbers can be multiplied together to give an odd number. Using the multiplication sign (×) to record number sentences	Pairs	Reasoning, problem-solving
Fruity problems (p35)		Drawing images to help solve word problems and using the multiplication sign to write calculations to represent the problems	Individuals	Problem-solving

Assessing progress

Use these questions (or similar) to help you assess children's understanding during and after these activities.

- *Can you write 5 + 5 + 5 + 5 as a multiplication sentence?*
- *Fill in the missing numbers 5 × 2 = _ , _ × 10 = 60, 10 × _ = 50.*
- *Can you make up a number story for 5 × 2?*
- *Can you write 6 lots of 2 as a multiplication?*
- *How many different multiplications can you make using the cards ×, =, 5, 10, 4, 20 and 2?*

INTRODUCING THE MULTIPLICATION SIGN

PAGES 20 TO 21

You need: a collection of paint brushes and paint pots

STEPS

- Place 4 paint pots on the table and put 2 paint brushes in each pot. Ask: *How many pots? How many brushes in each pot? Are the groups equal? How do you know?*

- Discuss different ways of representing the equal groups, for example with concrete apparatus such as cubes/counters, in pictures, in words (*4 groups of 2* or *4 lots of 2*), as a repeated addition (2 + 2 + 2 + 2). Model each strategy.

- Write 4 × 2 = 8 on the board. Explain that this is another way of representing that 4 groups of 2 equals 8. Say that the symbol × is called a multiplication sign.

- Repeat several times using different arrangements of paint brushes and paint pots. Model different vocabulary associated with the multiplication sign (for example *lots of*, *times*, *multiplied by*).

EXTEND

All children draw a picture that shows an equal grouping of objects (for example 5 vases each containing 2 flowers). They swap pictures with someone else in the group. Ask: *Can you write a multiplication to describe their picture?*
Mix up the pictures and number sentences. *How quickly can you match them together?*

COMPLETE THE TABLE

You need: resource 8 (Stools!); pencils

STEPS

- Look at resource 8 (Stools!) together. Look at and discuss the headings and the information in the first row of the table. Ask: *What does the picture show? Can you think of a different way of drawing 4 lots of 3? How could we write the multiplication in words?* (for example 4 groups of 3/4 times 3) *How would we write 4 groups of 3 as an addition sentence? How would we write a multiplication? How is 3 + 3 + 3 + 3 the same as 4 × 3?*

- Ask children to fill in the empty sections of the table. Discuss with them what they are doing, modelling the use of appropriate mathematical vocabulary, such as *times* or *lots of*.

- Ask children to compare answers with their neighbour. Ask: *Which of your answers are the same? Which are different? Why do you think this is?* (The answers in the first 2 columns may differ but the number sentences should be the same.)

EXTEND

Cut your completed table into sections. How quickly can you put it back together again? Can you use beads to calculate 3 × 2 =, 5 × 2 = , 3 × 5 = and so on?

TELL ME A STORY

You need: digital file 18 (Tell me a story)

STEPS

■ Display the problem in digital file 18 (Tell me a story): *I have 3 packets of sausages. There are 10 sausages in each packet. Which multiplication describes the number story correctly, 10 × 3 or 3 × 10?* Ask children to read it with their partner. Say: *Decide which number statement you think describes the story correctly and why.*

■ Share their answers. Encourage children to explain why 3 × 10 is the correct answer. Ask: *How do you know? Can you draw a picture to represent the problem? What does each number and symbol represent? Can you calculate the answer? How did you work it out?*

■ Ask: *How do you know 3 × 10 does not represent the story?* (there are not 10 groups with 3 in each group)

EXTEND

Write 5 different multiplications on the board. Relate a story for 1 of them. Ask: *Which multiplication sentence matches my story? How do you know?* Repeat, choosing different children to tell a number story each time.

Ask children to write and illustrate a number story for a given multiplication.

GETTING READY FOR WINTER

You need: digital file 19 (Getting ready for winter); a big bag of acorns or beads to represent acorns

STEPS

■ Display the word problem in digital file 19 (Getting ready for winter) and read it together: *Cyril the squirrel collected some acorns. He buried the acorns in the ground to keep them safe throughout the winter. Cyril dug 9 holes. He put 2 acorns in each hole. How many acorns did Cyril bury altogether?* Give each pair a pile of acorns and tell them to act out the story.

■ Choose 1 pair to demonstrate how they worked out the answer by grouping the acorns in 9 groups of 2. Work together to record the

calculation as a multiplication sentence on the board (9 × 2 = 18).

■ Make up different versions of the story for children to repeat the activity. Represent each story with a multiplication number sentence.

EXTEND

Children make up a number story for their partner to solve.

AM I RIGHT?

You need: digital file 20 (Am I right?); whiteboards and pens

STEPS

■ Display the number problem in digital file 20 (Am I right?):

5 + 5 + 5 + 5 + 5 + 5 = 6 × 5 Discuss the first question: *Is this correct?* Ask: *Do you think the answer is correct? How do you know?* (because 6 × 5 = 30 and 5 + 5 + 5 + 5 + 5 + 5 = 30) *What does each number and symbol represent? Can you use cubes to demonstrate to a partner that 5 + 5 + 5 + 5 + 5 + 5 is the same as 6 × 5?*

■ Ask children to write a multiplication sentence for each addition sentence. Share answers, inviting different children to explain them. Focus on 10 + 10 + 10 + 10 + 5 + 5 = Ask: *What is different about this addition sentence? Were you able to show this as a multiplication? What does your multiplication look like?* (5 × 10) *Why 5 × 10? I can only see 4 10s.*

EXTEND

Children practise writing other more complex addition sentences as multiplication sentences, for example 5 + 5 + 5 + 2 + 3 =

IF THIS IS THE ANSWER, WHAT IS THE QUESTION?

You need: digital file 21 (If this is the answer, what is the question?); counting apparatus

STEPS

■ Display the number problem in digital file 21 (If this is the answer, what is the question?): *The answer is an odd number. The question is a multiplication. What is the question?* Make sure children understand what they have to do. Ask: *What is an odd number? What is a multiplication? What does the multiplication sign look like? Do you think there will be more than 1 way to answer this question correctly? How do you know?*

■ Challenge children to come up with as many questions as they can, using the × sign. Observe how they tackle the problem; offer support and guidance as required. Make sure resources are easily accessible but let children make their own choices about what (if any) equipment they are going to use.

■ Discuss children's findings. Write a list of some of the possible questions on the board (for example 3 × 5 = 15, 1 × 3 = 3). Ask: *Can you explain why we were able to find so many possible answers?* (because there are many odd numbers)

EXTEND

Play a 'show me' game. Write a target number on the board. The first person to hold up a multiplication sentence that equals the target number is the winner.

FRUITY PROBLEMS

You need: resource 9 (Fruity problems)

STEPS

■ Give each child a copy of resource 9 (Fruity problems). Explain that you would like them to draw a picture to help them solve each problem. Demonstrate by working collectively to solve the first problem. Ask: *What do I need to draw first?* (3 bowls) *How many apples do I need to draw in each bowl?* (5 apples) *How can I use my picture to calculate the total number of apples? How should I count the apples?* (in 5s) *What is the answer to the problem?* (15 apples)

■ Now work together to write a multiplication calculation to describe the image (3 × 5 = 15). Ask: *What does this calculation mean? What does each number and symbol represent?*

■ Ask children to draw images to help them solve the remaining problems on resource 9 (Fruity problems). For the problems involving measures rather than an amount of objects, you could demonstrate how to annotate the images, for example write '2' on the front of each juice carton to show that it contains 2 litres.

EXTEND

Children write 3 more fruity problems for a partner to solve.

2-, 5- AND 10-TIMES TABLES

By the end of Year 2, children should be able to recall and use multiplication facts confidently for the 2-, 5- and 10-multiplication tables. This section contains activities and games to develop fluency with multiplication facts for the 2-, 5- and 10-times tables. It also provides real-life problem-solving activities in which children are given opportunities to apply multiplication in other areas of maths, such as money and measures. Using concrete objects, pictures, arrays and number lines, children explore equal groups within the 2-, 5- and 10-times tables. They identify patterns and make connections between these tables, for example the 10-times table doubles the 5-times table. The activities also include the commutative property of multiplication, usually covered in Year 2. Note: this section has been sub-divided according to the times table focus, however many activities can be adapted to use with the times table of your choice.

What multiplication do these shapes show? How many lots of 5?
How much altogether? Can you show me this another way?

Assessing progress

Use these questions (or similar) to help you assess children's understanding during and after these activities. Adapt to focus on the times table of your choice.

- *What is 5 × 2/4 lots of 2/6 multiplied by 2?*
- *How many gloves in 7 pairs?*
- *How many 2s make 10?*
- *If double 11 is 22, what is 2 × 11?*
- *What is 6 × 5/7 times 5/0 lots of 5?*
- *How many sides on 9 pentagons?*
- *A cinema ticket costs £5. I spend £25. How many tickets do I buy?*
- *If 6 × 5 equals 30, what else do you know?*
- *Is 40 a multiple of 5? How do you know?*
- *What is 4 ×10/9 × 10/7 lots of 10?*
- *There are 10 pencils in a box. How many pencils are there in 7 boxes?*
- *How many 10p coins are there in £1?*
- *Can you draw an array to show 4 × 10 equals 10 × 4?*
- *Fill in the missing numbers: 7 × 2 = ☐, ☐ × 5 = 15, 4 × ☐ = 20*
- *How many 2p/5p/10p coins could you exchange for a 50p coin?*
- *Would you rather have 10 2p coins or 5 5p coins?*

Test multiplying by 2, 5 and 10

The 2-times table

Activity	Objective	Focus	Organisation	Development
Bus queue (p37)	Calculate mathematical statements for multiplication and division within the multiplication tables and write them using the multiplication (×), division (÷) and equals (=) signs (Year 2)	Practising calculating the 2-times table using concrete apparatus	Whole class/ small groups	Fluency
Tell me a story (p38)		Practising calculating the 2-times table using arrays	Pairs	Fluency
Bang the drum (p38)		Introducing children to the 2-times table	Whole class	Fluency
Problem-solving (p38)	Solve problems involving multiplication and division, using materials, arrays, repeated addition, mental methods, and multiplication and division facts, including problems in contexts (Year 2)	Solving multiplication word problems	Pairs	Problem-solving, fluency
True or false? (p39)	Recall and use multiplication and division facts for the 2-, 5-, and 10-multiplication tables, including recognising odd and even numbers (Year 2)	Reasoning about number patterns within the 2-times table	Whole class	Problem-solving, reasoning
Speedy show me (p39)			Whole class	Fluency
Roll it 2! (p40)		Developing quick recall of multiplication facts for the 2-times table	Pairs	Fluency
Skittles (p40)			Small groups	Fluency
2-times table bingo (p40)			Whole class/ groups	Fluency

BUS QUEUE

PAGES 22 TO 23

You need: a large object to act as a bus stop; small play people

STEPS

■ Choose 4 volunteers to make a queue at the bus stop. Ask: *How many people are waiting at the bus stop? How many feet are waiting at the bus stop?* Observe how children count the feet. Do they count in 2s or do they count in 1s? Can they explain why they chose to count in 2s? Discuss why it can be useful to count larger sets of objects in groups.

■ Say together, *4 lots of 2 makes 8.* Record this as a number sentence on the board (4 × 2 = 8). Make sure that children understand what each number and symbol in the calculation represents.

■ Choose a different number of children to stand at the bus stop and repeat the activity.

■ Give each small group a set of play people. Ask them to make their own bus queues with different numbers of people and write a multiplication calculation to represent the number of feet each time.

EXTEND

Practise quick recall of multiplication facts for the 2-times table. Tell children how many people are standing in the bus queue. How quickly can they calculate the total number of feet? Let children investigate simple problems, for example *There are 8 feet waiting at the bus stop. How many people are waiting at the bus stop altogether?*

TELL ME A STORY

You need: whiteboards and pens

STEPS

■ Write 8 × 2 = ☐ on the board. Ask: *What does the 8 represent? What does the 2 represent? What does × mean?* (multiplied by, times, lots of)

■ Tell a number story for 8 multiplied by 2, for example *There are 8 rabbits in the pet shop. Each rabbit has 2 ears.*

■ In pairs, children draw an array to represent the story. Ask them to describe how they use the array to calculate 8 lots of 2.

■ Write 6 × 2 = ☐ on the board. Children think of a number story for 6 × 2 and draw an array to represent it. Invite pairs to tell their story. *What is 6 × 2? Describe your array and explain how it helped you calculate the answer.*

EXTEND

On squared paper, children colour an array for each multiplication fact for the 2-times table (1 × 2 to 12 × 2).

BANG THE DRUM

You need: a small drum and beater

STEPS

■ Write 5 × 2 = ☐ on the board. Ask: *What does each number and symbol represent? What different strategies could we use to help us work out the answer?* (for example counting 5 lots of 2, drawing a picture or array, making 5 jumps of 2 on the number line)

■ Use the drum to help the class calculate 5 lots of 2. Strike the drum 5 times, as children count on in 2s. Record the answer (10) on the board.

■ Now write 7 × 2 = ☐ Ask: *How many lots of 2 do we need to count to calculate the answer?* The child who gives the correct answer can beat the drum 7 times as the rest of the class count in 2s. Discuss: *How did the drum help us calculate the answer? What else could we use to keep track of the number of 2s we have counted?* (fingers)

■ Repeat for other calculations in the 2-times table.

■ Finally, ask children to look at all the calculations recorded on the board. Ask: *What do you notice about the multiplications?* (all the numbers have been multiplied by 2) Explain that all the facts make up the 2-times table and that children will learn to recall these facts from memory.

EXTEND

Swap the drum for a different percussion instrument and practise facts for the 5- and 10-times tables.

PROBLEM-SOLVING

You need: digital file 22 (Problem-solving); cubes; counters; resource 10 (Problem-solving)

STEPS

■ Display digital file 22 (Problem-solving) and read the word problem: *There are 11 bikes leaning on the wall. How many wheels?* Ask: *How could we work out the answer?* Model different strategies children suggest (for example drawing wheels, using cubes or counters to represent wheels, recall of known number facts). Ask: *How could we record the calculation as a number sentence?* (11 × 2 = 22)

■ Children solve as many of the problems on resource 10 (Problem-solving) as they can. They should write a number sentence to show the calculation used to solve each problem. Observe children as they collaborate on the task. Do they use practical strategies to calculate the answer or are they beginning to recall the number facts for the 2-times table from memory?

■ As a class, share answers to the problems. Ask: *What do you notice about the calculations?* (they are all number facts for the 2-times table)

EXTEND

Quick finishers can write a problem for their partner to solve.

TRUE OR FALSE?

You need: digital file 23 (True or false?)

STEPS

■ Display digital file 23 (True or false?) and read through the first part of the word problem: *Eleni is learning number facts for the 2-times table. Help her fill in the missing numbers in the following calculations. 3 × 2 = __ , 5 × __ = 10, __ × 2 = 8* Discuss what the numbers and symbols in each calculation represent. Fill in the missing numbers together. Encourage children to recall the facts from memory if they can. Then ask them to model the answer using a particular method, for example *Can you tell me a story that illustrates 5 × 2 = 10 is correct? Can you use an array to demonstrate that 4 × 2 = 8?* Model the use of mathematical language, such as *times, lots of, multiplied by, total*.

■ Encourage children to think of other facts for the 2-times table and record them on the board.

■ Now look at the second part of the problem: *Will the answers always be even when she multiplies by 2? Why do you think this?* Let children discuss ideas in pairs. Ask: *Do you think this statement is true or false? Can you explain your reasoning?* (I know if I count in 2s I will always land on an even number. The answers in the 2-times table grow by 2 each time. If I count on in 2s from 2, I will always land on a multiple of 2. Multiples of 2 are all even numbers.)

EXTEND

Write a list of missing number problems on the board for children to solve. Discuss: *Is every even number a multiple of 2? How do you know?*

SPEEDY SHOW ME

You need: number cards (even numbers to 24) for each child

STEPS

■ Ask children to look at their number cards. Ask: *Can you arrange them in order from smallest to largest? What do you notice about the numbers?*

■ Call out a calculation from the 2-times table (for example 5 × 2). Ask children to show the answer by holding up the correct number card. Discuss the different strategies children may have used to calculate the answer (for example recall, looking at the number line, using their fingers). Repeat for other calculations in the 2-times table.

■ Play 'speedy show me'. Call out calculations from the 2-times table. Ask children to hold up the correct answer as quickly as they can.

■ Gradually increase the pace of questioning as children develop quicker recall of number facts.

EXTEND

Play the game to practise facts for the 5- and 10-times tables.

ROLL IT 2!

You need: resource 6 (Roll it!); game board; 2 1–6 spot dice; 2 sets of different coloured counters

STEPS

■ With resource 6 (Roll it!), player 1 chooses whether to roll 1 or both dice. They multiply the total number of spots by 2 and then cover the total on their game board with 1 of their counters.

■ Children take turns to play. If a player makes a number, for example 4, and all the 4s on the board have already been covered, they miss a turn. They continue until 1 of them has covered 4 counters in a row.

■ Talk to children while they are playing and ask questions to develop understanding. *Are there any numbers on the board you will not be able to cover? Which numbers? How do you know? Where would you like to put your next counter? What number do you need to roll to allow you to cover the number 6, 8 etc? Are you going to roll 1 or both dice on your next go? Explain why.*

EXTEND

The game board can easily be adapted to practise multiplication facts for the 5- or 10-times tables.

SKITTLES

You need: 10 skittles; 3 small balls; a small cone or marker (per group)

STEPS

■ Set up the skittles in an area with the cone placed a short distance in front of the skittles to act as a marker to stand behind.

■ Tell children to try and knock down as many skittles as they can by rolling 3 balls at the skittles, 1 at a time. They score 2 points for each skittle knocked down.

■ Ask them to calculate their score: *How many skittles have you knocked down?* (for example 7) *What is 7 lots of 2?* If children can't recall the number fact from memory, they can work out their score by counting on in 2s as they touch each skittle knocked down. They record their score.

EXTEND

Ask children to use the scoring information to answer questions, for example *Mollie scored 14 points. How many skittles did she knock over? Who knocked down 10 skittles? How do you know?*

2-TIMES TABLE BINGO

You need: a bag containing small cards showing multiplication calculations for the 2-times table (1×2 up to 12×2)

STEPS

■ Write the multiples of 2 to 24 on the board. Tell children to choose 6 of these numbers and write them on a piece of paper to create a bingo card.

■ Draw a card out of the bag and read out the calculation (for example 3×2). Ask children to work out the answer in their head. Say: *If you have written 6 on your bingo card, you may cross it out.*

■ Talk about strategies children might use to help them work out the answer if they are unable to recall the number fact from memory.

EXTEND

In small groups, children can play a different version of the game using cards with the multiplication calculations for the 5- and 10-times tables. Children take turns to be the bingo caller.

The 5-times table

Activity	Objective	Focus	Organisation	Development
Pentagon, pentagon, pentagon (p42)	Calculate mathematical statements for multiplication and division within the multiplication tables and write them using the multiplication (×), division (÷) and equals (=) signs (Year 2)	Calculating the 5-times table using concrete apparatus	Whole class/ pairs	Fluency
Christmas decorations (p42)		Using knowledge of the 5-times table facts to solve a problem	Individuals	Fluency
How old? (p43)	Solve problems involving multiplication and division, using materials, arrays, repeated addition, mental methods, and multiplication and division facts, including problems in contexts (Year 2)	Using knowledge of facts for the 5-times table to solve a problem	Whole class/ pairs	Reasoning, problem-solving
Paint pots (p43)			Small groups	Reasoning, problem-solving
What do you notice? (p44)		Using knowledge and understanding of the 5-times table to reason about odd and even numbers	Whole class/ small groups	Reasoning, problem-solving
Hard and easy (p44)	Show that multiplication of 2 numbers can be done in any order (commutative) and division of 1 number by another cannot (Year 2)	Developing children's understanding that multiplication of 2 numbers can be done in any order	Whole class	Reasoning, problem-solving
Musical times tables (p45) **5-times table facts** (p45)	Recall and use multiplication and division facts for the 2-, 5-, and 10-multiplication tables, including recognising odd and even numbers (Year 2)	Developing quick recall of multiplication facts for the 5-times table	Whole class	Fluency

PENTAGONS, PENTAGONS, PENTAGONS

PAGES 24 TO 25

You need: a bag containing plastic or cardboard pentagons; a simple screen

STEPS

■ Remove a pentagon from the bag and hold it up. Ask: *What shape is this?* (a pentagon) *How do you know?* (It has 5 sides. It has 5 corners.)

■ Choose a volunteer to take 3 pentagons out of the bag. Ask: *How many pentagons? How many sides? How did you calculate the total number of sides? Who counted in 1s? Who counted in 5s? Can you explain why?*

■ Say together, *3 lots of 5 makes 15*. Record this as a number sentence on the board ($3 \times 5 = 15$). Make sure that children understand what each number and symbol represents.

■ Using different volunteers, take different numbers of pentagons out of the bag and repeat the activity several times. In pairs, children write a multiplication calculation to represent the total number of sides for each set of pentagons.

EXTEND

Hide some of the pentagons behind a screen. Tell children how many sides the pentagons have altogether. Ask: *How many pentagons have I hidden behind the screen? How do you know?*

CHRISTMAS DECORATIONS

You need: resource 11 (Christmas decorations); counting equipment (for example cubes; counters)

STEPS

■ Give each child resource 11 (Christmas decorations). Say: *Look at the Christmas tree. Count how many of each decoration have been used to decorate the tree. Fill in the first column of the table.*

■ Children then work out how many of each type of decoration they would need to decorate 5 identical trees. They record their answers in the table.

■ Observe how children calculate the answers. Do they count in 5s or are they beginning to recall multiplication facts for the 5-times table from memory? Let children use concrete apparatus if they want to.

■ Look at the competed tables. Share answers. Invite different children to describe how they worked out the answers using appropriate mathematical vocabulary (for example *multiplied by*, *lots of*, *times*).

EXTEND

Children solve simple word problems involving multiplication facts for the 5-times table, for example *If 8 teams entered the 5-a-side football tournament. How many players were there altogether?*

HOW OLD?

You need: digital file 25 (How old?)

STEPS

■ Display the word problem on the board from digital file 25 (How old?) and read it together: *Josh is 5. Josh's brother Oliver is 3 times Josh's age. Dad is 8 times Josh's age. Grandpa is 12 times Josh's age. How old is each person in Josh's family?*

■ Encourage children to describe in their own words what the problem is asking. Ask: *What is the key piece of information that will help you solve the problem? Do you think you will need to add, subtract or multiply to work out the age of each family member? Why?*

■ Let children solve the problem, recording their working as number sentences, for example Oliver is 3 times as old as Josh who is 5 so Oliver is $5 + 5 + 5$, or 3×5.

■ Gather the class together to discuss answers. Ask: *What are the ages of Oliver, Dad and Grandpa? How did you work it out? Which times table did you find useful?*

EXTEND

Set other simple word problems that require children to draw on their knowledge of the 2-, 5- and 10-times tables. Ask them to make up a word problem for a partner to solve.

PAINT POTS

You need: digital file 26 (Paint pots); Number tracks; whiteboards and pens; cubes

STEPS

■ Display digital file 26 (Paint pots), read and discuss the word problem: *A decorator needs 43 litres of paint. Can she buy the exact amount of paint she needs? How do you know? How many pots of paint should she buy? Will she have any paint left over? How much?* Ask: *Do you think the decorator will be able to buy the exact amount of paint? Explain your reasoning.* (She will not be able to buy the exact amount of paint because 43 is not in the 5-times table. 43 is not a multiple of 5.)

■ Let children work out how many pots of paint the decorator needs to buy. (9)

■ Choose different children to explain how they calculated the answer. Ask: *How much paint will be left over? How do you know?*

EXTEND

Set other simple problems, for example *You need 59 litres of paint. How many pots should you buy? How much will you have left over?* or *I need 37 litres of paint. I buy 7 pots. Do I have enough paint? How many more litres do I need?*

WHAT DO YOU NOTICE?

You need: digital file 27 (What do you notice?); cubes

STEPS

■ Display digital file 27 (What do you notice?) and read the first part of the problem together: *Multiply all the even numbers to 12 by 5.* Discuss what it is asking children to do.

■ In groups of 2 or 3 children, multiply all the even numbers to 12 by 5 and record their answers. Ask: *How many different calculations have you written?* (there should be 6) *Are you sure you have got them all? Explain how you know. What do you notice?* (All the numbers end in 0. The answers are all multiples of 10. They are all even numbers.) *Can you explain?* (for example 2 lots of 5 make 10 so every time you add an even number of 5s it will make a multiple of 10)

■ Now read the second part of the problem: *What do you notice? Can you explain? What do you think will happen if you multiply all the odd numbers to 11 by 5?* Encourage children to describe in their own words what they think might happen if the odd numbers to 11 are multiplied by 5. What pattern might they expect to see? Why do they think this?

■ In groups, children multiply all the odd numbers to 11 by 5. Ask: *What do you notice? Is this the pattern you expected to see?*

EXTEND

Ask: *Can you tell me a 3-digit number that, when multiplied by 5, would give an answer ending in 0? Explain how you know. If I divide 310 counters into groups of 5, will I have an odd or even number of groups? How do you know?*

HARD AND EASY

You need: digital file 28 (Hard and easy)

STEPS

■ Display digital file 28 (Hard and easy) and discuss the word problem together: *Ben is trying to work out the answer to 5 × 12. He is finding it tricky to count in 12s. What could he do to make it easier to find the answer?* Ask children to suggest how Ben could make it easier to work out the answer to 5 × 12.

■ Discuss their ideas (for example use apparatus to make 5 groups of 12; draw a picture or an array; swap the numbers in the multiplication around to make 12 × 5 because it is easier to count in steps of 5 than 12; 12 × 5 is equivalent to 5 × 12).

EXTEND

Ask: *Can you make an array to show 3 × 11 is the same as 11 × 3?*

MUSICAL TIMES TABLES

You need: a cymbal and a beater; number cards; whiteboards and pens

STEPS

■ Call out a multiplication calculation from the 5-times table (for example 10 × 5).

■ Strike the cymbal. Challenge children to write the answer to the calculation on their whiteboards before the cymbal stops ringing.

EXTEND

Ask: *How many multiplication facts for the 5-times table can you write before the fidget spinner stops spinning or the sand timer runs out?*

5-TIMES TABLE FACTS

You need: number cards (multiples of 5 up to 60); a number square

STEPS

■ Ask each pair to spread their number cards face down on the table.

■ Children take turns to turn over a card. They race to be the first player to say what number must be multiplied by 5 to make this total. The winner keeps the card. If they disagree they can use a number square to help them decide on the correct answer.

■ Discuss with children what they are doing and provide support where necessary. Can they describe the strategy they are using to work out the answer? (for example recall, counting on fingers)

■ Once all the cards have been won, they count to see who has collected the most.

EXTEND

Children use a mixed set of number cards (multiples of 2, 5, and 10). They think of a multiplication calculation in the 2-, 5- and 10-times tables which makes the number on the card they have selected.

The 10-times table

Activity	Objective	Focus	Organisation	Development
In the ring (p47)	Solve 1-step problems involving multiplication and division, by calculating the answer using concrete objects, pictorial representations and arrays with the support of the teacher	Using concrete apparatus to calculate number facts for the 10-times table	Groups	Fluency
Coin purse (p47)	Solve problems involving multiplication and division, using materials, arrays, repeated addition, mental methods, and multiplication and division facts, including problems in contexts (Year 2)	Calculating number facts for the 10-times table and writing them out using the multiplication (×) and equals (=) signs	Whole class/ pairs	Fluency
Pizza toppings (p47)		Using knowledge of the 10-times table to solve a problem	Individuals	Fluency
True or false? (p48)		Providing an opportunity for children to develop their understanding of and ability to reason about patterns within tables with a focus on the 10-times table	Whole class/ pairs	Reasoning, problem-solving
Cover up (p48)	Recall and use multiplication and division facts for the 2-, 5-, and 10-multiplication tables, including recognising odd and even numbers (Year 2)	Developing quick recall of multiplication facts for the 10-times table	Pairs	Fluency
Park the car (p49)			Whole class in the playground or hall	Fluency
Jump in (p49)			Whole class standing in a circle	Fluency
Changing places race (p49)			Whole class standing in a circle with 2 children in the middle	Fluency

IN THE RING

PAGES 26 TO 27

You need: large hoops; beanbags; score sheet

STEPS

■ Nominate 1 child to stand a small distance away from the hoop. Ask them to try to throw 10 beanbags into the hoop. They score 10 points for each beanbag that lands in the hoop.

■ Ask: *How many beanbags have landed in the hoop?* (for example 4) *What is 4 lots of 10? How do you know?*

■ Demonstrate how to calculate the score by lifting the beanbags out of the hoop 1 at a time and counting in 10s.

■ Let each child have several turns. As you discuss what they are doing, model a variety of mathematical language (*multiplied by, lots of, times*).

■ The child with the highest score at the end of the game is the winner.

EXTEND

Let children investigate the question: *I scored 80 points. How many beanbags did I get in the hoop? How do you know?*

Children play variations of the game to practise calculating number facts for the 2- and 5-times tables. They throw balls into a bucket; score 2 points for each ball into a bucket. They kick footballs into a net; award 5 points for each goal scored.

COIN PURSE

You need: a small purse; 10p coins; whiteboards and pens

STEPS

■ Place 6 10p coins in the purse. Say: *There are 6 10p coins in the purse.*

■ In pairs, children work out how much the coins in the purse are worth altogether. They record their answer on their whiteboards.

■ Discuss and compare some of the strategies that children used to calculate the answer. Encourage the use of a range of mathematical language to describe multiplication (*multiplied by, lots of, times*).

■ Choose a child to tip the coins out of the purse and count in 10s to check the total value. Record it as a multiplication calculation (6 × 10p = 60p). Discuss what each symbol and number represents.

■ Repeat the activity varying the number of coins in the purse each time.

EXTEND

Let children solve some simple problems, such as: *The total value of the 10p coins in the purse is 80p. How many coins are in the purse altogether?*

☐ × 10 = 80

PIZZA TOPPINGS

You need: resource 13 (Pizza toppings)

STEPS

■ Ask children to look at the pizza on resource 13 (Pizza toppings). They carefully count how many pieces of each topping are on the pizza and record their answers in the table.

■ Say: *Imagine you work in a pizza takeaway. Someone has ordered 10 of these pizzas. Work out how many pieces of each topping you will need to make 10 pizzas exactly the same as the 1 in the picture.* Children record their answers in the table.

■ Observe how children calculate the answers. Do they count in 10s or can they recall multiplication facts for the 10-times table? Are any children still choosing to use concrete apparatus or pictorial representations?

■ Look at the completed tables. Share children's answers. Invite different children to describe how they worked out the answers using appropriate mathematical vocabulary (*multiplied by, lots of, times* and so on).

EXTEND

Quick finishers could design a different pizza and calculate the number of each topping they would require to make 10 pizzas.

Ask: *Can you calculate how many pieces of each topping you would need to make 2 pizzas? What about for 5 pizzas?*

TRUE OR FALSE?

You need: digital file 29 (True or false?)

STEPS

■ Display digital file 29 (True or false?). Look at the first part of the problem: *5 × 10 = 10 × 5* Ask: *Is this true or false? How do you know?* Draw a 5 × 10 array on the board to illustrate that the multiplication of 2 numbers can be done in any order (commutative). Ask children to suggest other multiplication facts for the 10-times table which show the commutativity of multiplication (for example 3 × 10 = 10 × 3; 4 × 10 = 10 × 4).

■ Look at the second part of the problem:
7 × 10 = 10 + 10 + 10 + 10 + 10 +10
10 × 2 = 2 × 10
10 + 10 + 10 + 10 = 4 × 10
1 × 10 = 5 × 2
2 × 10 = double 2
Let children spend a few minutes looking at each statement with a partner before discussing as a group. Encourage different children to explain their reasoning each time.

■ 2 of the answers are false
(7 × 10 = 10 + 10 + 10 + 10 + 10 + 10 and 2 × 10 is double 2). Challenge children to change 1 side of each equation to make the statements true.

EXTEND

Ask: *How many different ways can you represent, for example 8 lots of 10?*

COVER UP

You need: 2 number strips each marked with the multiples of 10 up to 100; number cards (1–10); 20 counters

STEPS

■ Look together at the number strip. Ask: *What do you notice about the numbers?* (They are all multiples of 10. They all end in 0.) Count in unison in 10s from 10 to 100 and back again. Ask children to describe the number sequence.

■ Children play 'cover up'. They shuffle a set of number cards and place them face down on the table. Player 1 turns over the top card, multiplies the number on the card by 10 and then covers the answer on their number strip with a counter.

■ The aim is to be the first player to cover up all of the numbers on their number strip. When all the number cards have been turned over once, they shuffle the pack and begin again.

■ Ask children questions to assess their understanding, for example: *What number card would you need to turn over to be able to cover 50? Explain how you know. How could you check your partner has covered the correct number on the number strip? Do you notice anything about the number on the card and the multiple of 10 you have covered?*

EXTEND

Adapt the game for children to practise times tables facts for the 2- and 5-times tables.

PARK THE CAR

You need: large number cards (multiples of 10 up to 120)

STEPS

■ Spread the number cards face up around the school hall.

■ Children should imagine that the hall is a giant car park and each number represents a parking space. Ask them to pretend that they are driving around looking for a space to park but unfortunately all the spaces are full.

■ You are the car park attendant. You will let children know when a space becomes free by calling out a calculation, for example 5×10. Children calculate the answer and 'drive' to the correct space (number card) as quickly as they can.

EXTEND

Play the game again to practise the 2- and 5-times tables. Turn the activity into a knock-out game. The last child to get to the correct parking space each time is out. Continue to play until only 1 driver remains.

JUMP IN

You need: several sets of number cards (multiples of 10 to 120)

STEPS

■ Give each child a number card.

■ Call out a calculation from the 10-times table, for example 11×10. Children jump into the middle of the circle if they are holding the answer (110) and sit down.

■ Repeat with different calculations until everyone has jumped in and is sitting down.

■ Children swap number cards. This time, repeat the activity but children blast off like a rocket if they are holding the answer.

EXTEND

Each child holds a card with a calculation (for example 5×10). They jump into the circle if you call out the answer to their calculation. Alternatively, they throw a beanbag into the circle if they are holding the answer to a calculation.

CHANGING PLACES RACE

You need: large number cards (repeated multiples of 10, 1 per child)

STEPS

■ Give each child a number card and tell them to place their card face up on the floor in front of them.

■ Call out a 10-times table calculation, for example 7×10. The 2 children in the middle must race to find the answer. Whoever locates the correct number first (70) swaps places with the child with that number.

■ Repeat until everyone has had at least 1 turn in the middle.

■ If necessary, remind children of different strategies they could use to help them calculate the answer if they are unable to recall the number facts from memory (for example making 7 jumps of 10 on a number track or a 100 square).

EXTEND

Adapt the game to practise facts for the 2- and 10-times table at the same time. Play with 3 children in the middle who all have to race to find the answer. Instead of calling out calculations, set simple times tables word problems, for example: *If 5 children jump into the swimming pool. How many toes altogether?* or *If 4 children are watching TV. How many eyes are there?*

Mixed times tables

Activity	Objective	Focus	Organisation	Development
Coin exchange (p51)	Solve problems involving multiplication and division, using materials, arrays, repeated addition, mental methods, and multiplication and division facts, including problems in contexts (Year 2)	Using repeated addition to solve multiplication problems set in a money context	Whole class/ individuals	Reasoning, fluency
Treasure Island (p51)	Calculate mathematical statements for multiplication and division within the multiplication tables and write them using the multiplication (×), division (÷) and equals (=) signs (Year 2)	Multiplying numbers by 2, 5 and 10	Individuals	Fluency
Multiplication chain (p51)	Recall and use multiplication and division facts for the 2-, 5-, and 10-multiplication tables, including recognising odd and even numbers (Year 2)	Developing understanding of a variety of language related to multiplication and relate times tables facts for the 2-, 5- and 10-times tables to grouping, arrays and repeated addition	Pairs	Fluency
Equals, greater or less than? (p52)	Solve problems involving multiplication and division, using materials, arrays, repeated addition, mental methods, and multiplication and division facts, including problems in contexts (Year 2)	Multiplying numbers by 2, 5 and 10 and using the symbols = < > to compare mathematical statements	Whole class/ pairs	Reasoning, problem-solving
Dice challenge (p52)	Recall and use multiplication and division facts for the 2-, 5-, and 10-multiplication tables, including recognising odd and even numbers (Year 2)	Developing quick recall of multiplication facts for the 2-, 5- and 10-times tables	Whole class in small groups	Fluency
It's a knockout! (p53)			Whole class	Fluency
Goal! (p53)			Whole class in 2 teams	Fluency
Race to 100 (p53)			Small groups	Fluency

COIN EXCHANGE

PAGES 28 TO 31

You need: coins (£1, 50p, 20p, 10p, 5p, 2p, 1p); resource 14 (Coin exchange)

STEPS

■ Together, look at the coins. What is the value of each coin? Pose some simple multiplication problems such as: *I have 5 10p coins. How much money have I got altogether? I have 12 2p coins. How much money have I got altogether?*

■ Use the coins to practise exchanging coins of the same value. Ask: *How many 1p/2p/5p coins could I exchange for a 10p coin? How many 1p/2p/5p coins could I swap for a 20p coin? How do you know?*

■ Hand out resource 14 (Coin exchange). Ask children to explore ways of exchanging a 50p coin or a £1 coin.

EXTEND

Children could find different ways of exchanging a £2 coin.

TREASURE ISLAND

You need: resource 15 (Treasure Island); coloured crayons; number lines; counting apparatus

STEPS

■ Ask children to look at the pirates' treasure map on resource 15 (Treasure Island). They must follow the clues to find where the pirates have buried their treasure.

■ Ask children to solve the first clue: *8 × 2.* Some may be able to quickly recall the number fact from memory, others may use practical methods. Choose different children to demonstrate the strategy they used (for example concrete apparatus, drawing an array, repeated addition, jumps on a number line).

■ Tell children to locate the answer (16) on the grid and to mark the square with a coloured cross.

■ Working independently, children solve the remaining clues and cross out the corresponding squares on the map. They will find the treasure buried in the 1 square on the map that is not crossed out.

EXTEND

Children draw their own treasure map, decide where to bury their treasure and write a list of clues to lead their partner to the treasure.

MULTIPLICATION CHAIN

You need: resource 16 (Multiplication chain); scissors

STEPS

■ Ask each pair to cut out the cards on resource 16 (Multiplication chain). Tell children to find the start card and solve the multiplication: *3 lots of 2.* They find the answer on 1 of the other cards, then answer the next question and so on. Explain that if all the questions are answered correctly the cards will form a loop.

■ Support children as they complete the task. Ask questions to assess their understanding such as: *What is another way of writing 6 groups of 2? Can you think of a different multiplication question with the answer 14?*

EXTEND

As a class, how quickly can children order an enlarged set of the cards on resource 16 (Multiplication chain)? Remove 1 of the cards from the chain. Can children design a new card that could go in that space?

EQUALS, GREATER OR LESS THAN?

You need: digital file 30 (Equals, greater or less than?)

STEPS

■ Display digital file 30 (Equals, greater or less than?) and look at the questions together. Discuss what each symbol (<, >, =) means.

■ In pairs, children look at the first question. They decide whether to use <, > or = to make the statement correct. Ask: *Explain how you worked out the answer. What does this statement show us?* (multiplication of 2 numbers is commutative meaning it can be done in any order) Ask: *Can you think of other multiplications that are equal to 4 × 5?* (2 × 10, 20 × 1 and so on)

■ Ask children to use <, > or = to complete the other statements. Share answers. Choose a different child to explain their reasoning for each answer.

EXTEND

Write a list of questions on the board, for example
3 × 5 = ☐
7 × 10 = ☐
2 × 2 = ☐ and so on. Children think of a multiplication fact to complete each statement.

DICE CHALLENGE

You need: a 1–9 dice; a dice labelled 2, 2, 5, 5, 10, 10; shuffled number cards (0–100)

STEPS

■ Pick a number card at random and stick it on the board. Children take turns to roll both the dice and multiply the 2 numbers together (for example 9 × 2).

■ Record each child's score in a table on the board.

■ The child who has made the number closest to the picked number is the winner and scores a point. Ask: *Would it be possible to make the exact number on the card by multiplying 2 of the numbers on the dice together? If not, what is the closest number you can make?* Award a bonus point to the first child to make the target number or the closest possible.

■ The winner is the child with the most points at the end of the game.

EXTEND

Investigate: *What numbers would you need to roll on the dice to score a total of 35 points? How many different ways could you score 20 using these dice?*

IT'S A KNOCKOUT!

You need: stickers, merits or other small rewards

STEPS

■ Choose 2 volunteers to stand up and face each other.

■ Call out a multiplication from the 2-, 5- or 10-times tables, for example 7×2. The children standing up should shout out the answer as quickly and loudly as they can. The first to call out the correct answer is the winner. Their opponent is knocked out of the game and must sit down.

■ Use the activity to model a variety of mathematical language, for example 7×2 could be 7 *lots of* 2, 7 *times* 2, 7 *multiplied by* 2, *double* 7.

■ Award a sticker or small prize if a certain goal is reached, for example if a contestant knocks out 5 opponents in a row.

EXTEND

Children race to be the first to solve a simple multiplication problem, such as: *I ate 2 apples every day last week. How many apples did I eat altogether?* Call out a multiple of 2, 5 or 10. Children race to be the first to call out a multiplication calculation which makes that number.

GOAL!

You need: 10 blue counters; 10 red counters; material for sticking counters on the board

STEPS

■ Name 1 team 'The Blues' and the other 'The Reds'. Draw a large set of goalposts on the board.

■ Say that the aim of the game is to be the first team to score 10 goals.

■ Nominate 1 player from each team to take a shot at the goal. Call out a multiplication calculation from the 2-, 5- or 10-times tables, for example 5×10. The first player to shout out the correct answer (50) scores a goal for their team. Stick a red/blue counter inside the goalposts to record which team scored.

■ Continue playing until 1 team has scored 10 goals.

EXTEND

Children play the game in pairs using cards showing assorted multiplication calculations from the 2-, 5- and 10-times tables.

RACE TO 100

You need: game boards made by shading 30 random squares on a 100 square; a 1–6 dice; counters; sets of question cards (multiplication questions from the 2-, 5- and 10-times tables)

STEPS

■ Children place a coloured counter of their choice on number 1 on the game board.

■ They take turns to roll the dice and move their counter the appropriate number of spaces on the board. If a player lands on a shaded number square, they should turn over a question card. The first member of the group to answer the question correctly moves their counter forward 3 spaces.

■ The winner is the first player to reach 100.

EXTEND

Use question cards with 2-step multiplication problems for example (double 5) $\times$ 10 or $(2 \times 5) \times 5$.

HALVING

Before teaching children how to halve a number it is essential that they understand that halving means splitting an object, shape or quantity into 2 equal parts. Sometimes, when used in everyday conversations, we don't always mean to halve in equal parts and this can be confusing. In Year 1, children are introduced to fractions and taught to find and name a half as 1 of 2 equal parts of an object, shape or set of objects. This can be demonstrated practically by dividing a variety of everyday objects, pictures and shapes into 2 equal pieces. The activities in this section focus on teaching children how to find half of sets of objects and numbers. Children are shown how to use concrete resources to find half of a small number or quantity by equal sharing or grouping, how to halve a larger number using partitioning, and are introduced to the concept that halving is the inverse of doubling.

 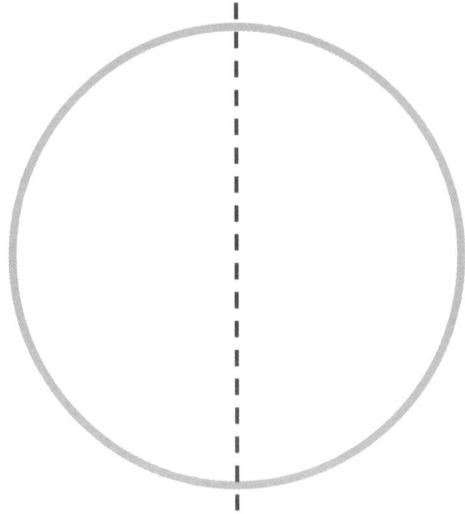

Sam says he ate half his lunch. Lucy says this circle is split in half.
What is the same? What is different?

Activity	Objective	Focus	Organisation	Development
Play date (p56)	Solve 1-step problems involving multiplication and division, by calculating the answer using concrete objects, pictorial representations and arrays with the support of the teacher	Using concrete resources to find half of a number by equal sharing	Whole class/ pairs	Fluency
Train fares (p56)	Solve problems involving multiplication and division, using materials, arrays, repeated addition, mental methods, and multiplication and division facts, including problems in contexts (Year 2)	Learning how to halve a 2-digit number by partitioning	Whole class/ individuals	Reasoning, problem-solving
What's my number? (p57)		Choosing a suitable halving strategy to solve a number problem	Whole class/ pairs	Reasoning, problem-solving
Target number (p57)		Practising doubling and halving small numbers	Pairs	Reasoning

Assessing progress

Use these questions (or similar) to help you assess children's understanding during and after these activities.

- *Share 10 cubes with a partner. How many cubes do you each get?*
- *Share 12 flowers equally between 2 vases. How many flowers are in each vase?*
  Draw a picture to help you find the answer.
- *What is half of 18?*
- *If double 3 is 6, what is half of 6?*
- *I am thinking of a number. If I halve it the answer is 11. What is my number?*
- *What is the opposite of halving? Give me an example of both using a number of your choice.*

Test multiplying and dividing by 2

PLAY DATE

PAGES 32 TO 33

You need: a selection of small toys (for example cars, trains, bricks, cubes, counters); resource 17 (Play date)

STEPS

■ Choose 3 children to act out a simple story: *2 children are playing with some cars. 1 of them starts to cry. He runs off to find his dad. What do you think is the matter?* Explain that he is upset because he hasn't got as many cars as his friend. Ask: *What could Dad do to sort out the problem?* (He could share the cars out equally between the 2 children.)

■ Tell 'Dad' to share the cars equally between the 2 children. Ask: *How many cars has each child got?* (for example 4) *How many cars are there altogether?* Explain that when we share a set of objects equally between 2 people they each get half of the objects. Ask: *What is half of 8?*

■ Repeat for a different scenario choosing different children to act out the problem.

■ Hand out resource 17 (Play date). Ask children to use practical apparatus to halve each number.

EXTEND

Children solve simple halving problems by drawing pictures or a bar model to find half of a number by equal sharing.

TRAIN FARES

PAGES 34 TO 35

You need: digital file 31 (Train fares); resource 18 (Train fares); small whiteboards and pens; base 10 apparatus

STEPS

■ Display digital file 31 (Train fares). Ask children to talk to their neighbour about the problem: *A return rail ticket from London to Brighton costs £46. A 1-way ticket costs half that amount. How much does a 1-way ticket from London to Brighton cost?* Ask: *How could you work out the answer? What equipment could you use to help you?*

■ Allow children a few minutes to try and solve the problem before asking them to share their answers. Establish that the answer is £23. Ask children who answered correctly to describe how they worked the answer out (for example sharing 46 cubes into 2 equal piles, using base 10 to halve the number). Explain that some strategies, such as sharing objects into 2 groups become less efficient when working with larger numbers. Focus on partitioning strategies. Demonstrate how to halve 46 using both base 10 equipment and a halving wall to partition and recombine the numbers. Ask: *How can we check we have halved the number correctly?* (double our answer)

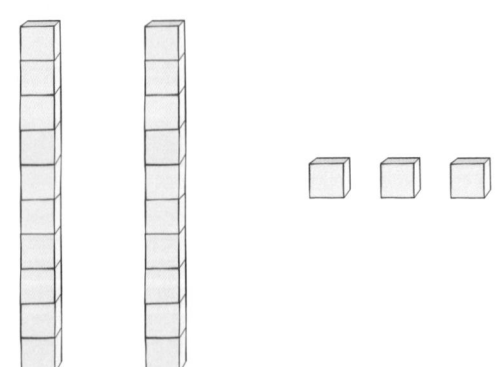

■ Hand out resource 18 (Train fares) and ask children to halve the price of each return ticket using 1 of the partitioning strategies you have demonstrated.

EXTEND

Children use partitioning to halve a 3-digit number.

WHAT'S MY NUMBER?

You need: digital file 32 (What's my number?); small whiteboards and pens; practical apparatus (cubes, counters)

STEPS

■ Display digital file 32 (What's my number?) and read the first word problem together: *I think of a number then double it. The answer is 22. What is my number?* Can children explain in their own words what the problem is asking them to do?

■ In pairs, let children choose their own equipment to help them work out and check their answer. Encourage them to represent their answer on a whiteboard (for example with a picture, number sentence, halving wall). Listen carefully to them as they discuss the problem; provide support where necessary.

■ Share answers. Invite pairs to demonstrate how they worked their answer out.

■ Now ask children to solve the second word problem in the same way: *I think of a number, then double it and double it again. The answer is 16. What is my number?*

EXTEND

Repeat with larger numbers. Children pick a number and write a similar riddle for their partner to solve.

TARGET NUMBER

PAGE 41

You need: 100 squares; number lines; counters; 1–6 dice

STEPS

■ Children choose a target number on their 100 square and mark it with a counter. Their aim is to land exactly on the target number.

■ Explain the rules of the game. Children play in turn. Player 1 rolls the dice and decides whether to double or halve the number. Player 2 does the same. Player 2 must then choose whether to add or subtract their number to or from Player 1's number.

■ The resulting number becomes the running total. On each turn, the players use the running total to add or subtract their number to or from, until 1 player lands on the target number and wins the game.

■ Ask children to suggest how they could keep track of their running total during the game (for example writing it down, placing a second counter on the 100 square).

■ Observe children as they play and offer support and guidance as necessary.

■ This game can be simplified by giving children a smaller range of numbers to choose from (for example using a 0–20 number line).

EXTEND

Children play the game with 2 dice to practise doubling and halving numbers to 12.

9

DIVISION

I n Year 1, children are taught to use objects and pictorial representations to solve simple problems involving division by sharing or grouping, without using the division symbol. Children need to understand the difference between division by *sharing*, for example *Share 8 balloons equally between 2 children* and division by *grouping*, for example *How many groups of 5 can you make from these 15 counters?* A number of the activities in this book can be easily adapted to develop children's early understanding of division by grouping, for example *Snack time*, *Sorting sheep* and *Grabbing game* (Section 3) and *Bead strings* (Section 4). Children are usually formally introduced to the topic of division in Year 2. They are taught how to read, write and interpret mathematical statements involving division using the division ($\div$) and equals ($=$) signs. Children will investigate patterns in the multiplication tables including finding fact families, for example $5 \times 2 = 10$, $2 \times 5 = 10$, $10 \div 2 = 5$, $10 \div 5 = 2$. They will also begin to realise that division is not commutative.

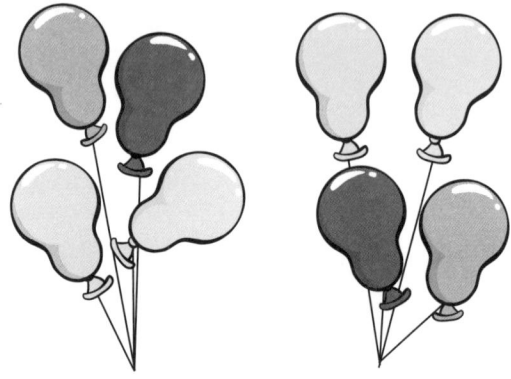

I share 8 balloons between 2 children. There are 4 balloons in each group.

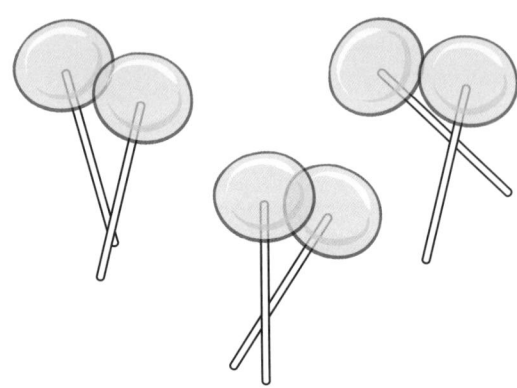

I divided 6 lollies into groups of 2. There are 3 groups.

Activity	Objective	Focus	Organisation	Development
Sharing sweets (p60)	Calculate mathematical statements for multiplication and division within the multiplication tables and write them using the multiplication ($\times$), division ($\div$) and equals ($=$) signs (Year 2)	Practising calculating the 2-times table using concrete apparatus	Whole class/ small groups	Fluency
Sharing marbles (p60)	Solve problems involving multiplication and division, using materials, arrays, repeated addition, mental methods, and multiplication and division facts, including problems in contexts (Year 2)	Using properties of odd and even numbers to solve a problem	Whole class/ pairs	Reasoning, problem-solving
Sorting socks (p61)	Calculate mathematical statements for multiplication and division within the multiplication tables and write them using the multiplication ($\times$), division ($\div$) and equals ($=$) signs (Year 2)	Using practical apparatus to work out how many groups are in a given number. Beginning to use the division ($\div$) and equals ($=$) signs to record division calculations.	Whole class/ groups	Problem-solving

Activity	Objective	Focus	Organisation	Development
At the bakery (p61)	Calculate mathematical statements for multiplication and division within the multiplication tables and write them using the multiplication (×), division (÷) and equals (=) signs (Year 2)	Using pictorial representations to divide a number of objects by grouping. Using the division (÷) and equals (=) signs to record division calculations.	Whole class/ groups	Problem-solving
Dividing on a number line (p62)	Calculate mathematical statements for multiplication and division within the multiplication tables and write them using the multiplication (×), division (÷) and equals (=) signs (Year 2)	Using a number line to divide a number of objects by grouping. Using the division (÷) and equals (=) signs to record division calculations	Groups	Fluency
Problem-solving (p62)	Solve problems involving multiplication and division, using materials, arrays, repeated addition, mental methods, and multiplication and division facts, including problems in context (Year 2)	Beginning to choose own methods and equipment to solve problems	Whole class/ pairs	Problem-solving, reasoning
The crown jewels (p63)		Choosing and using practical apparatus to group a set of objects	Pairs	Reasoning, problem-solving
Flower beds (p63)	Show that multiplication of 2 numbers can be done in any order (commutative) and division of 1 number by another cannot (Year 2)	Recognising that division will start with the larger number while the multiplication of 2 numbers can be in any order	Whole class and individuals	Reasoning
Am I right? (p64)	Solve problems involving multiplication and division, using materials, arrays, repeated addition, mental methods, and multiplication and division facts, including problems in contexts (Year 2)	Beginning to see a link between multiplication and division	Whole class/ pairs	Reasoning, problem-solving
Number sentences (p64)	Calculate mathematical statements for multiplication and division within the multiplication tables and write them using the multiplication (×), division (÷) and equals (=) signs (Year 2)	Using ÷, ×, = signs to record multiplication and division calculations	Individuals	Reasoning

Assessing progress

Use these questions (or similar) to help you assess children's understanding during and after these activities.

- *Share 10 cubes equally between 2 people. How many will they each have?*
- *Can you use apparatus to work out how many groups of 2 there are in 20?*
- *Count in 5s to 25. How many 5s have you counted?*
- *Fill in the missing numbers: $30 \div 10 = \boxed{}$, $\boxed{} \div 2 = 5$, $50 \div \boxed{} = 10$.*
- *Can you write 2 division sentences to describe this array?* (show image of for example 5 rows of 2 counters)
- *If $8 \times 2 = 16$, what is $16 \div 2 = ?$*
- *If double 10 is 20, what is half of 20?*

Test multiplying and dividing by 2, 5 and 10

SHARING SWEETS

You need: large sorting hoops; 3 cuddly toys; 3 paper plates; wrapped sweets or cubes; a paper bag

STEPS

■ Place 2 of the toys in the circle with a plate beside each toy. Explain that the toys have been given a bag of 10 sweets and they need some help to share them equally.

■ Choose a child to practically share the 10 sweets between the 2 toys. Ask: *How do you know you have shared the sweets equally? How many sweets did the toys have to share? How many groups did you share the sweets into? How many sweets did each toy get? Can you fill in the missing numbers? 10 sweets can be shared into* ☐ *equal groups of* ☐.

■ Now choose a different child to share 12 sweets equally between 3 toys. Ask: *How many sweets did each toy get? Can you fill in the missing numbers?* ☐ *sweets can be shared into* ☐ *equal groups of* ☐.

■ Repeat several more times varying the number of sweets and/or toys each time.

EXTEND

Children investigate what happens if they try to divide an odd number of objects into equal groups. Ask: *What do you notice?* (sometimes there are too many objects/not enough to make a whole group)

SHARING MARBLES

You need: digital file 33 (Sharing marbles); cubes; whiteboards and pens

STEPS

■ Display digital file 33 (Sharing marbles) and read the problem together, then discuss it: *Sally and Jim want to buy a bag of marbles. They want to buy a bag of marbles that they are able to share equally with none left over. Which bag of marbles should they buy?* Ask: *Which bag of marbles do you think the children should buy so that they can share them equally? Can you explain why?* (The bag with 24 marbles because it is an even number and can be shared into 2 groups with no marbles left over. 25 and 29 are odd numbers and I know an odd number of objects cannot be shared equally into 2 groups.)

■ Children draw a picture to represent the equal groups. Ask: *How many marbles will Sally and Jim get? How do you know?*

■ Now ask the pairs to investigate how many marbles the children would each get if they shared them with 2 more of their friends. Can they demonstrate the strategies they used to work out and check their answer?

EXTEND

Set other simple problems, such as: *If 5 children share a bag of 25 sweets equally how many will they each get? Could 3 children share a bag of 14 marbles equally between them? Why not?*

SORTING SOCKS

PAGES 36 TO 37

You need: a basket containing 12 pairs of socks; cubes; whiteboards and pens

STEPS

■ Show children the basket full of socks. Choose a child to count the total number of socks (24). Tell the group you would like to know how many pairs of socks there are. Ask: *How could we find out?* (by grouping the socks in 2s)

■ Pick a child to act out the problem by arranging the socks in pairs. Ask: *How many socks were in the basket? How many socks in each pair? How many pairs altogether? How many groups of 2 are there in 24? How do you know?*

■ Introduce the division symbol. Demonstrate how to record the information as an abstract number sentence using the division and equals symbols: $24 \div 2 = 12$. Explain how the division statement shows how many 2s there are in 24 and that 24 items can be divided into 12 groups of 2.

■ Make up similar problems for the groups to solve, such as: *There are 14 socks in the basket. How many pairs?* Children work out the answers using practical equipment (for example cubes to represent socks). They work together to write a division statement to represent each problem.

EXTEND

Discuss: *How can the 2-times table help you when dividing by 2?*

AT THE BAKERY

You need: digital file 34 (At the bakery); cubes; whiteboards and pens

STEPS

■ Display digital file 34 (At the bakery) and read the first word problem together: *A baker baked 35 rolls. She put 5 rolls in each bag. How many bags did she fill?* Ask: *What do we need to find out? How many rolls has the baker made? How many is she going to put in each bag or group? What equipment could we use to help us?* (for example cubes or counters)

■ Allow children a few minutes to solve the problem practically.

■ Display the second problem and count the rolls together. Discuss how the image might be used to work out the answer (for example ring the 35 rolls in groups of 5 and then count up the number of groups).

■ Choose children to ring the rolls in groups of 5. Ask: *How many groups of 5 are there in 35? How do you know? How would we write this as a division?* ($35 \div 5 = 7$) *Can you write a multiplication to describe the problem?* ($7 \times 5 = 35$) *What do you notice about the number sentences?* Explore how the 2 calculations are linked.

EXTEND

Make up other similar problems for children to solve, such as: *The baker baked 20 cakes. She put 2 cakes in each box. How many boxes did she fill?* Ask children to draw a picture to help them work out the answer.

DIVIDING ON A NUMBER LINE

You need: blank number lines; 10p coins; a pot; cubes; whiteboards and pens

STEPS

■ Hold up a pot of coins. Say that you have been collecting 10ps and you have a total of 60p.

■ Ask the groups to choose 1 piece of equipment and use it to work out how many 10ps are in the pot. Ask them to describe how they calculated the answer (for example using real coins, drawing pictures of coins, counting in 10s using their fingers, making jumps of 10 on a number line).

■ Draw a number line on the board. Demonstrate how to work out how many 10s in 60 by making equal jumps along the number line.

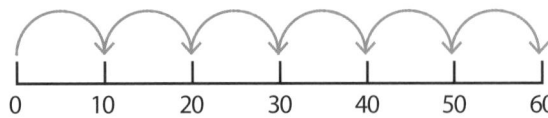

■ Pick a child to draw jumps of 10 to 60 on the number line. Ask: *What does the number line show? How many 10s in 60? How do you know?* (I counted the number of jumps we made.) Ask children to write a matching division calculation. (60 ÷ 10 = 6)

■ Repeat with a different number of 10ps in the pot. Ask children to draw jumps on a number line and then to show the division as a number sentence.

■ Repeat several times with different numbers of 10ps.

EXTEND

Adapt the activity by using 5ps or 2ps to practise dividing by 5 or 2 on a number line.

PROBLEM-SOLVING

You need: digital file 35 (Problem-solving); blank number lines; cubes; counters

STEPS

■ Display digital file 35 (Problem-solving) and read the word problem together: *Mr Black bought 45 rubbers. There were 5 rubbers in each pack. How many packs did he buy?* Ask children to talk with their neighbour about what the word problem is asking.

■ Discuss the problem together. Ask: *What do you need to find out?* (how many rubbers are in each pack) *What do you already know?* (the number of packs; the total number of rubbers)

■ Observe how children approach the activity in their pairs, providing support and guidance where necessary. Encourage them to select an appropriate problem-solving strategy and method of recording their working (for example as jumps on a number line or as a number sentence).

■ Invite children to describe how they calculated the answer and recorded their working (for example using concrete apparatus, drawing pictures, jumps on a number line). Ask: *If you were to solve a similar problem would you choose the same strategy or equipment? Why?*

EXTEND

Set other word problems for children to solve independently, such as: *Mr Black bought 60 rulers. There were 5 in each pack. How many packs did he buy? Mrs Green spent £15 on books. Each book cost £5. How many did she buy?*

THE CROWN JEWELS

You need: digital file 36 (The crown jewels); blank number lines; cubes; counters

STEPS

■ Display Digital file 36 (The crown jewels). Children read the problem: *I have between 15 and 30 jewels. If I divide the jewels into 5 equal groups I have 2 jewels left over. How many jewels do I have?* and discuss with their partner what they think the problem is about. Ask: *What do you know? What do you need to find out? Do you think there might be more than 1 solution? Talk about the methods they could use to solve the problem and how they could record their answers.*

■ Allow children time to solve the problem, encouraging them to make their own decisions about what strategies and equipment they use and how they record their answer.

■ Discuss what they have found out. Ask: *Does everyone have the same answer(s)?* (there could be 17, 22 or 27 jewels in the chest) *How do you know you have found all the answers? Did you test all the numbers or did you spot a pattern?* (the answers are all multiples of 5 + 2)

■ Compare the different methods children used to solve the problem. Ask: *If you were asked to solve a problem like this again would you do anything differently? Why?*

EXTEND

Set a similar problem in a different context, for example *Harry collected a bucket of shells. If he divides them into groups of 5 he has 2 left over. If he divides them into groups of 3 he has 1 left over. What is the smallest number of shells he could have in his bucket?*

FLOWER BEDS

You need: digital file 37 (Flower beds); whiteboards and pens

STEPS

■ Display digital file 37 (Flower beds) and look together at the 3 × 10 flower bed array. Ask: *How many rows and columns of flowers are there? How many flowers are in each row or column? How many flowers are there altogether?* Ask children to write 2 multiplication facts to describe the array (3 × 10 and 10 × 3). Talk about what these calculations show us. (multiplication of 2 numbers can be done in any order)

■ Working together, write a division fact to describe the array. Circle the flowers in the flower bed into groups of 10 to show the division clearly. Ask: *How can we show this as a number sentence?* (30 ÷ 10 = 3)

■ Tell children you are going to swap the numbers round to make a second division fact: 10 ÷ 30 = 3. Can children spot a problem? (It is not possible to divide 10 flowers into groups of 30.) Circle the flowers in groups of 3. Can children show the division as a number sentence on their whiteboards?

■ Emphasise that although the multiplication of 2 numbers can be done in any order, the division of 1 number by another cannot. Ask: *What do you notice about the 2 sentences?* (both start with the larger number) *Can you explain why?*

■ Display the second screen and ask children to write 2 multiplication and division facts to describe the flower bed/s. (10 × 5 = 50; 5 × 10 = 50; 50 ÷ 10 = 5; 50 ÷ 5 = 10)

EXTEND

Ask: *How many different number sentences can you write using these numbers and symbols: 4 20 5 = × ÷ ?*

AM I RIGHT?

You need: digital file 38 (Am I right?); small whiteboards and pens; practical apparatus (for example cubes, counters)

STEPS

■ Display digital file 38 (Am I right?) and discuss the first statement: *If a number ends in 0 it always divides exactly by 5.* Ask: *What does it mean? Do you think it is correct? Can you explain why?* (I know that all numbers that end in 0 are a multiple of 5 because I say these numbers when I count in 5s. I know that 5 + 5 = 10 and so any number that ends in 0 will divide into groups of 5.)

■ In pairs, children use equipment to find evidence to support these answers.

■ Then consider the second statement: *I can use 5 times table facts to help me divide by 5.*

■ Write the following number sentences on the board:

40 ÷ 5 =

10 ÷ 5 =

20 ÷ 5 =

5 ÷ 5 =

Ask: *What is 4 × 5?* (20) *Which division question on the board does this fact relate to?* (20 ÷ 5) *What is the answer? How do you know?* (If 4 lots of 5 is 20, I know that 20 can be divided into 4 groups of 5.)

■ Repeat for the other number sentences. Ask: *Do you think knowing number facts for the 5-times table can help you divide by 5? Can you give reasons for your answer?*

EXTEND

Ask: *Can you write a dividing rule for a different set of numbers? For example if a number ends in 0, then it always divides exactly by what?*

NUMBER SENTENCES

You need: counting apparatus; resource 2 (100 square); number lines

STEPS

■ Write this list of symbols and numbers on the board: 1 2 3 4 5 10 10 20 30 40 50 ÷ × =

■ Discuss what the symbols ÷, × and = mean. Challenge children to use the numbers and symbols to make as many different number sentences as they can.

■ Observe children working. Are they looking for 1 number sentence at a time or are they looking for related multiplication and division facts (for example 5 × 10, 10 × 5, 50 ÷ 10, 50 ÷ 5)?

■ Gather children together and share answers. Ask: *Has anyone organised their number sentences in groups? Can you explain how you did this and why?* (for example I know that multiplication of 2 numbers can be done in any order so as 4 × 10 = 40, I know 10 × 4 = 40. I know that division is the inverse of multiplication so 40 ÷ 10 = 4 and 40 ÷ 4 = 10.)

EXTEND

Ask: *Can you write a number sentence which contains all 3 symbols?* (for example 20 × 3 ÷ 2 = 30)